PREACHING ON THE SAYINGS OF JESUS

MOWBRAY PREACHING SERIES

Series editor: D. W. Cleverley Ford

PREACHING ON THE SAYINGS OF JESUS

D. W. CLEVERLEY FORD

MOWBRAY

Mowbray
A Cassell imprint
Wellington House, 125 Strand, London WC2R 0BB
215 Park Avenue South, New York, NY 10003

First published 1996

British Library Cataloguing-in-Publication Data
A catalogue record for this book is available from the British Library.

ISBN 0-264-67416-2

Typeset by Keystroke, Jacaranda Lodge, Wolverhampton
Printed in Great Britain by Biddles Ltd, Guildford and King's Lynn

CONTENTS

ACKNOWLEDGEMENTS

May I express my appreciation of the encouragement given me by Ruth McCurry, Religious Editor of Cassell, to write this book, and to Miss Barbara Hodge for producing such an excellent typescript from my handwritten MS – not easy to read, but over the years she has grown used to its idiosyncrasies.

D. W. Cleverley Ford
Lingfield 1995

THE SAYINGS

1 THE GOSPEL OF ST MARK

1 Change your minds   Mark 1.15 (NEB)
*The time has come; the kingdom of God is upon you; repent,
and believe the Gospel.*

2 Hearing is basic   Mark 4.23 (NEB)
If you have ears to hear, then hear.

3 The liberal approach   Mark 9.40 (NEB)
For he who is not against us is on our side.

4 Divorce   Mark 10.9 (RSV)
*What therefore God has joined together, let not man put
asunder.*

5 The wealthy   Mark 10.25 (NEB)
*It is easier for a camel to pass through the eye of a needle than
for a rich man to enter the kingdom of God.*

6 Concerning ambition   Mark 10.43 (NEB)
Whoever wants to be great must be your servant.

7 Imaginative prayer   Mark 11.24 (NEB)
*I tell you, then, whatever you ask for in prayer, believe that
you have received it and it will be yours.*

8 Our two debts   Mark 12.17 (NEB)
*Pay Caesar what is due to Caesar, and pay God what is due
to God.*

9 The resurrection of the dead   Mark 12.27 (NEB)
God is not God of the dead but of the living.

2 THE GOSPEL OF ST MATTHEW

10 Love your enemies   Matthew 5.44 (RSV)
Love your enemies and pray for those who persecute you.

11 How not to pray   Matthew 6.7 (NEB)
In your prayers do not go babbling on like the heathen, who imagine that the more they say the more likely they are to be heard.

12 Be careful about seeing   Matthew 6.22 (NEB)
The lamp of the body is the eye.

13 The mastery of worry   Matthew 6.34 (AV)
Sufficient unto the day is the evil thereof.

14 The exercise of discrimination   Matthew 7.6 (AV)
Give not that which is holy unto the dogs, neither cast ye your pearls before swine, lest they trample them under their feet, and turn again and rend you.

15 Good foundations   Matthew 7.24 (RSV)
Every one then who hears these words of mine and does them will be like a wise man who built his house upon the rock.

16 The extent of God's care   Matthew 10.29–31 (NEB)
Are not sparrows two a penny? Yet without your Father's leave not one of them can fall to the ground. As for you, even the hairs of your head have all been counted. So have no fear; you are worth more than any number of sparrows.

17 Jesus religion   Matthew 11.28–30 (RSV)
Come to me, all who labour and are heavy laden, and I will give you rest. Take my yoke upon you, and learn from me; for I am gentle and lowly in heart, and you will find rest for your souls. For my yoke is easy, and my burden is light.

18 Bad language, good language   Matthew 12.33 (NEB)
You can tell a tree by its fruit.

3 THE GOSPEL OF ST LUKE

19 A rich fool   Luke 12.14 (RSV)
Man, who made me a judge or divider over you?

20 A hard saying   Luke 12.51 (RSV)
*Do you think that I have come to give peace on earth? No,
I tell you, but rather division.*

21 Religious pride   Luke 14.11 (RSV)
*For every one who exalts himself will be humbled, and he
who humbles himself will be exalted.*

22 The family   Luke 14.26 (NEB)
*If anyone comes to me and does not hate his father and
mother, wife and children, brothers and sisters, even his own
life, he cannot be a disciple of mine.*

23 God and money   Luke 16.13 (AV)
*No servant can serve two masters: for either he will hate the
one, and love the other; or else he will hold to the one, and
despise the other. Ye cannot serve God and mammon.*

24 Lost and saved   Luke 19.10 (RSV)
For the Son of man came to seek and to save the lost.

INTRODUCTION

The sayings of Jesus are not the foundation of the Christian gospel, the foundation is the cross of Christ. It is what he did for us there that impels us to enquire what he was like and what he said. It is not unfitting, therefore, that I should make bold to follow up my three books, *Preaching the Risen Christ*, *Preaching on the Crucifixion* and *Preaching on the Historical Jesus*, with the present volume, *Preaching on the Sayings of Jesus*. The sayings do not come first, but they must come. They are bound to come. Insistent as we must be that what Jesus did for us has the priority, the question is certain to arise, 'What did he say?'

Furthermore, in the second quarter of the first century, as Christian assemblies began to spring up in response to the gospel, that is the good news of Jesus Christ's life laid down for us, it was inevitable that guidance should be sought on what Christians should believe and how they should behave; and where would be the obvious place to look first of all for this but in the way Jesus was seen to live and in what he said, indeed in the teaching of Jesus himself?

Jesus was a teacher. He was commonly known as The Teacher, often called Rabbi. This is how he was remembered. And we must not forget that he was a public figure. Thousands upon thousands of people must have both seen him and heard him in Judaea and Galilee. And they would remember his sayings. He intended that they should be remembered. They were cast in memorable form and with memorable language, not a little of it with poetical structures reminiscent of the literary style prominent in the Old Testament. These striking sayings and extended teaching sessions would be recalled after he was crucified – years after – and collected. Various collections were made, and from these the four gospels we have in the New Testament were constructed incorporating 'the sayings', and not only incorporating them but arranging some of them so as to make discourses, notably 'the Sermon on the Mount' so called, and also setting them in their original context where they were first uttered. To observe this is important. Each saying arose out of a 'life situation', what the Germans call the '*Sitz im Leben*'. This being so, the context of each saying must receive attention if its meaning is to be grasped. And the preacher must give skilled attention to it, and re-present it in his sermon. This has been attempted in this book.

It will be noticed that all the sayings commented on in the sermons are derived from the first three gospels, the synoptic gospels as they are commonly designated. And so the well-known 'I am' sayings of Jesus, as they are called, seven in St John's gospel, receive no attention. There is a reason for this. The fourth gospel, St John's, was written later than the first three, and of these St Mark's was the earliest. They are therefore closer in time and closer to the original 'life situation' in which the sayings were uttered. This does not guarantee their authenticity, but it does mean that in the fourth gospel the words of Jesus have been filled out and interpreted by the writer, not distorting them but drawing out a deeper significance than was evident in the original setting. A rough-and-ready way to understand this is to conceive of the synoptic gospels as providing a *photograph* of Jesus speaking on a number of occasions and the fourth gospel as providing an artist's *portrait* of Jesus on other occasions. A portrait does not distort, it draws on a depth of appreciation that cannot be present in a photograph. Both have their part to play, but they must not be confused with each other.

There is also this difference to be noted with regard to the sayings of Jesus. What is given in the synoptic gospels is largely, though not altogether, his words to the multitudes as they are called, mixed assemblies of people, many of whom could be roughly categorized as 'outsiders'. The situation in the fourth gospel is different. There we find Jesus engaged either in confrontation with skilled opponents of his ministry, or in close and intimate communion with his disciples and others sympathetic to him in heart and mind.

So it is that the cryptic sayings of Jesus are to be found in the synoptic gospels and not in the fourth, and so framed and worded as to intrigue and capture the attention of the hearers, leaving them wondering and thinking, if not distinctly puzzled. This fact alone made the sayings memorable. They were not forgotten when they were uttered, some of them over and over again, and never have been forgotten. This is why they are a proper subject for preaching in any age. The sayings are also a distillation of his person. As we listen to the sayings we can feel the presence of him who uttered them. Fortunate indeed is the congregation whose preacher on the sayings of Jesus so presents them that hearers can sense the divine presence. If my book helps at least a little in this, I ask no more.

D.W.C.F.
1995

1
CHANGE YOUR MINDS

The time has come: the kingdom of God is upon you; repent,
and believe the Gospel.
MARK 1.15 (NEB)

Change your minds! According to St Mark, those were the
first words that the people in Galilee heard Jesus proclaim.
Change your minds! But you look at me, the preacher,
puzzled, and I am not surprised. You have just heard my text
'The time has come; the kingdom of God is upon you;
repent, and believe the Gospel.' Was not his first word
'repent', not 'change your minds'? So I have to tell you that
the word for 'repent' in the Greek text is *metanoeite*, which
means 'change your minds'. So this really was the opening
appeal to the people flocking to see him, and hear him in
Galilee. 'Change your minds!' I know we don't like changing our minds, men especially; women do it more easily, they
don't at once count it as weakness; it may indeed be wisdom.
After all, there is no sense in hanging on to a position out of
sheer woodenness. Change your minds then, you people
of Galilee. This is how Jesus opened his ministry. And come
to think of it, Jesus would hardly draw attention if his very
first word was 'repent'; this would be much too severe, and
in any case there have to be antecedents before repentance
is possible. A preacher doesn't begin with repentance, that
comes later.

And what about the people listening? The Galileans
weren't all that religious, not like the people in Jerusalem
anyway; Galilee was the business end of Palestine. Trade
made it a mixed community. People were jostled together,
Jews with Gentiles, Gentiles with Jews, plus a considerable
mixture of Greek-speaking people, and of course Roman

1

soldiers belonging to the occupying force in the time of
Jesus. So ethnic tensions were only just below the surface.
Class distinction, however, was rare. There were the aristo-
cratic Sadducees and the ordinary people, this was all.
No middle class. It was into the maelstrom of ordinary
hopes, fears and expectations that Jesus came with his words,
'Change your minds.' I have good news for you about
God. And the extraordinary fact is the people listened. They
hung upon his words, and the basic reason was the speaker
himself.

1 THE SPEAKER IS THE MESSAGE

There must have been something about Jesus as a speaker.
For make no mistake, it is not simply what a speaker says
that opens ears, but the way he says it. More than that,
the speaker is the message before he opens his mouth at all.
People see his face, the brilliance or dullness of his eyes, the
set of his mouth. The speaker is the message. Is he a live
man? A strong man? A sensitive man? A compassionate man?
All such observations weigh heavily in the matter of giving
attention to a speaker. I have been reading in the news-
paper of new appointments to the Cabinet. I shall reserve my
judgement till I can see them, at least on television.

So when Jesus stood up among the working-class people
in Galilee, saying, 'Change your minds, I have good news for
you,' he must have looked like the bearer of good news.
There was a vitality about his presence and a directness
which told of action to be taken, something more than
words. They watched his face, they saw the sparkle in his
eyes, and noted the aliveness of his body. So they listened.
This speaker was gripping, almost like an entertainer.

I am stressing the fact that the speaker is the message
because in this course of sermons on the sayings of Jesus I
want to point out that the words are first of all a disclosure
of the speaker himself. It is a mistake to lift out of the gospel

2

narratives some of his arresting sayings like 'The lamp of the body is the eye' and then without more ado proceed to dissect them and apply them. All this will come later. First the question must be asked, 'What does this saying tell us about Jesus?'

When a new minister is appointed to a church many more people than usual turn up to hear the first sermon. But when they return home for Sunday lunch it is not the content of what the new minister said that they discuss, even if they remember it, but, 'What sort of man do you think we have among us? Shall we like him?'

2 THE CONTENT OF THE MESSAGE

And now back to the text, 'The time has come; the kingdom of God is upon you; change your minds, and believe the good news.' And what is the good news? It is that the time has come, the kingdom of God is upon you; you are in a new situation.

Now I would not be so foolish as a preacher to enter into the field of party politics, but one would have to be almost blind not to see that with the coming of Tony Blair on the scene we are in a new situation. The contours of the national situation have changed whether he becomes Prime Minister or not. And this is the point I would have you notice, the new situation has dawned because a *new person* is on the landscape. It is not first of all a new set of ideas or plans that creates a new environment, but a new leading figure. So, when Jesus made the announcement, 'the kingdom of God is upon you', that kingdom was present because *he was present* in their midst.

So what is the kingdom of God? Down in Jerusalem the religious leaders reckoned they knew. It was the nation of Israel called into being by God. They were proud of it, proud of themselves, God's chosen people! Their position was secure. What could Jesus possibly mean, pray, by saying,

3

'the time has come, the kingdom of God is upon you'? Was the Jewish nation about to be established in power and glory, with the hated Roman occupation come to an end? Or was he referring to the celestial kingdom about to be set up on earth? His hearers could not make out what he meant. And he obliged with no definition. All he said was the kingdom of God, the real presence of God, is here right now. Change your minds and believe this good news.

We ought to listen to this. Our tendency in thinking is to conceive of God as a superman up above the sky. This is quite wrong. God is a living presence in our midst now, close to our successes as well as our failures, closer than our hands and feet, longing for us to change our minds and believe this news about God, this gospel of God. And the wonder is that as the weeks and months rolled by, and the people in Galilee and beyond became acquainted with the new preacher and his wonderful works, they couldn't help but wonder if with Jesus in their midst God himself was not present, the real divine presence close at hand.

3 PREACHING IS MAKING GOD REAL

So what Jesus did first of all in his sayings was to make God real to his hearers. This is, or should be, the supreme task of every preacher. I am shy about saying this, although it is true, because I can't help wondering how far short of this has been my own ministry in the pulpit over the years. But this is the ultimate test of a preacher: does he make the presence of God credible? No, more than that: does he, does she, make the presence of God a reality, such a reality that the hearers sense it even if they do not wholly understand what is being said? What the preacher is in himself, herself, makes for this or does not make for it.

Not long after the First World War one called Canon Aubrey Aitken was Vicar of St Nicholas Church, Great Yarmouth, the second largest parish church in the county.

4

For most of the year this huge building was not filled with worshippers, but at the height of the summer it was crowded with holidaymakers, mostly from the industrial centres in the Midlands – Mum and Dad together with the family, come to spend their holidays 'on the sands' as they put it – and on Sundays they trooped into the Great Church which no one could possibly miss. And when at last Canon Aitken died, this is what I read about him in the *Eastern Daily Press*: 'For years from his pulpit he made God real to hundreds and hundreds of people who visited Great Yarmouth on holiday.' He did this as a preacher.

Jesus did this with his preaching, and not only with his preaching, but also by his many works of compassion, healing people and making them whole. With Jesus in their midst they could believe that God was present.

4 THE HEART OF PRAYER

And now I want to bring this home to us where we are. The *raison d'être* of prayer is not first of all to ask God for anything, or even to intercede for other people. It is to realize the presence of God, his real presence closer than our hands and feet, fully aware of our hopes and fears, and what we most desire. It is of this we must make ourselves aware when we kneel down to pray.

When I lived and worked in Lambeth Palace, the home and headquarters of the Archbishop of Canterbury, I soon became aware of how different the place felt when the Archbishop was not in residence, as was frequently the case, for he often took extended tours abroad. The full staff was busy about the palace, the heavy daily correspondence was dealt with as usual, visitors on various matters of business came and went, but the place was not the same. It was the presence of the Archbishop that made all the difference, we knew he was in that room at the top of the blue staircase immediately beyond the front entrance. I have no direct experience of a royal palace, but I can imagine how different everything must feel when the Queen is in residence and when she is not.

Can we really believe in the real presence of God in our midst? Life for most of us is a crowded out affair. Catching trains, answering the telephone, anxiously seeking a parking place for the car, standing in the shopping queue at the supermarket, getting the children off to school on time. Most of us can only just keep up with the pace of life today. How then can we come anywhere near the counsel of the psalmist, 'Be still and know that I am God'? It takes time to become still, it takes a concentration of the mind; but unless we reach that point when we kneel down for prayer, we have not really prayed, we have not made real the presence of God in our world. We shall almost certainly need help for this. A consecrated building set apart for prayer, a prayer book or manual in our hands, forms of prayer committed to memory, and for many the sacred elements of the Holy Communion set upon the altar. There will be different ways for different people, but when we do realize the divine presence close to us there will be nothing too ordinary, too human, too simple or too complicated that we need keep out of our prayers. So change your minds, the kingdom of God is upon you; repent and believe the gospel, the good news of his presence here and now. Jesus came to make this credible.

2

HEARING IS BASIC

If you have ears to hear, then hear.
MARK 4.23 (NEB)

What an odd summons! If you have ears to hear, then hear.
'If you have ears . . . ' Are there people then *without* ears?
Apparently there are, people without the faculty of hearing,
in other words deaf. To agree to this in the sphere of the
physical is not difficult. Some months ago I was invited to
stay in a house where lived an old lady over eighty. I had not
been told that she was becoming deaf, so I talked normally,
not raising my voice. But when she began answering
questions I had not asked, but thought I had, she was
embarrassed, noting the mystified look on my face. Of
course I 'tumbled to', as we say, and began speaking as if I
were in a pulpit without microphones. I felt sorry for her.
Deafness is not only limiting, it is isolating. Really deaf
people are lonely no matter how many people fill the room.
I have heard them say they would rather be blind than deaf.
I can't comment, but this I know: deafness is far more than
an inconvenience, it is a serious handicap. And this also I
know from the gospels, Jesus' heart went out to those lonely
people and he stretched forth his hands of healing.

1 SPIRITUAL DEAFNESS

But physical deafness is not the issue in my text, the words
of which Jesus repeated over and over again to the people
he was addressing, 'If you have ears to hear, then hear!' The

reference is to spiritual deafness. People there are, crowds of people, who have no ears for the spiritual in life at all. Their blank faces betray them when the subject is even hinted at. It doesn't mean anything to them. Jesus of course knew this. It was the same in his day, which is why he said, 'If you have ears to hear'. Some in the crowds he was addressing, perhaps many, were spiritually deaf. There was really little point in telling them about the kingdom of God. It was a waste of words. His concern had to be with those who could at least hear what he said. 'If you have ears to hear, then hear.'

Now the Bible from cover to cover lays much stress on hearing, spiritual hearing. You only need to pick up a concordance and note the multiplicity of references to ears and to hearing. And Jesus gave it the same prominence. It is not surprising therefore that in those Churches where the Bible is taken seriously hearing is a major element in the public worship. The worshippers are there to pray together, to sing together and to have fellowship one with another, but they are there to hear, indeed the words of Jesus are addressed to them specifically. 'If you have ears to hear, then hear.' We go to church to hear, or should do.

I am not sure that in the Church of England we haven't drifted away from this basic. Doing is what counts, doing good works, engaging in charitable exercises out of compassion for the unfortunate. And who shall say that such activity is not a proper concern of every Christian, indeed is a hallmark of the genuineness of the faith professed? By comparison hearing seems marginal. But is it? Some churches have answered 'Yes' by taking out the pews altogether. Those serried ranks of places to sit and listen offend the modern mood. Discussion in groups is the replacement, and a layout with moveable chairs able to be arranged in circles. This is the up-to-date approach in worship. The pulpit in front and the worshippers in fixed facing rows is considered restricting. Flexibility makes for vitality. Maybe, but does no hearing come in? And at the risk of being misunderstood, for *I* believe the Eucharist is central, I have to say that the use of the Parish Communion as the main service of worship on Sundays has in practice seriously minimized the hearing in the worship, and too often the sermon has been all but closed down as an act of importance.

'If you have ears to hear, then hear.' But the clergy and ministers must make it possible. I put this first because it would be wrong to lay all the blame for spiritual deafness upon the laity. Too often there is little to hear, little anyway to stimulate the mind and move the heart. Preachers are responsible for the worshippers' ability to hear, and I am not talking about volume of sound or even elocution, though both are important. I refer to *capturing attention* and holding it. Do you think the crowds were bored as they listened to Jesus' preaching? There would not have been those crowds if such had been the case. The truth is, they were gripped by his words, even if they often failed to understand them.

2 THE CAUSE OF SPIRITUAL DEAFNESS

And now the hard question: are some people *born* spiritually deaf? We know, sad to say, that some people are born *physically* deaf. They never did have the capacity to hear. But what about spiritual capacity? Is the situation the same here? I do not think so. Listen! Every child comes into the world with a sense of wonder. You can see it in the baby's eyes from very early on. There is wonder at any moving objects or creatures around the cot; and wonder when the first toy is given, and certainly for a girl a doll. Wonder arises from the sense of something beyond the self, something real though mysterious. It hits us all the more forcibly as we become aware of the great world around us, and in increasing degree as we become aware of the world of nature. Wonder is the seedbed of spiritual awareness in all of us. Its existence shows that we all are born with the capacity of spiritual hearing, we do 'have ears to hear'. And this conviction is buttressed by that striking verse in the first chapter of St John's gospel, which tells of the Word, or

9

Logos, as 'the true light that enlightens everyone born into this world'. Did you notice, 'enlightens everyone'? It is this then that makes the human being human. No, no one is *born* spiritually deaf, no one without ears to hear, but the trouble is they become blocked – sometimes, perhaps often, very quickly.

In the context of my text today, 'If you have ears to hear, then hear,' Jesus by means of a parable showed how this happens. By reason of the pressures of life people become like a pathway ceaselessly trodden over till it becomes as hard as if paved with stone. No matter what vital seed is cast upon it, nothing will grow, the ground cannot receive it. This is how people in the rush and tumble of life become spiritually deaf, they lose their ears for the spiritual, it is trampled on, even the tiny beginnings with which they were born. They never had a chance to grow. With some people the seed does begin to grow, but like a plant in shallow soil it soon withers away. And with other people all awareness of the spiritual dimension in life gets choked out of existence by the cares of the world and the persistent preoccupation with money, all too prevalent in today's world. So, sad to say, many people, young and old, even rich and poor, become deaf to the spiritual in life. They cannot hear, they have lost their ears. No amount of talking to them or preaching will have any effect. It simply passes them by.

3 HOW THOSE WHO CAN HEAR SHOULD HEAR

But what of those who can hear, even a little? What had Jesus to say to them? What has he to say to us? We turn again to the context of my text, Mark 4.24–25: 'Take note of what you hear; the measure you give is the measure you will receive, with something more besides. For the man who has will be given more, and the man who has not will forfeit even what he has.' So our manner of hearing is crucial to the kind of people we become. Congregations must not simply let the preaching flow over them. If it is a poor sermon, they must think out why they reckon it poor. If it is a good sermon, they must not treat it like a captivating play at the theatre, engrossing while it lasts but all but forgotten before they reach home. The mind must be given to hearing in church because it is the Word of God that is ministered, something of eternal consequence. People who hear it have their spiritual sensitivity quickened if they consciously give their mind to it. The more they give, the more they receive; the less they give, the more diminished they become in stature. This is true not only of individuals but of whole church congregations – the church where there is vigorous preaching and conscious deliberate hearing will be a strong church and the outcome will be not only intelligent spirituality but compassionate service of fellow men and women in need. Do I make my point? Proclaiming the Word of God is important, but so is hearing the Word of God. 'If you have ears to hear, then hear.' And 'take heed what you hear; the measure you give is the measure you will receive, with something more besides'. These are the sayings of Jesus.

4 CHRIST CAN OPEN DEAF EARS

But I haven't quite finished. Earlier on I said that if people are spiritually deaf, if they are as far as may be judged completely without ears for the hearing of the spiritual as opposed to the material and sensual, it is useless even trying to talk to them, let alone preach. Was this too sweeping? Yes, it was. Miracles can happen. Jesus' miracles of healing of the deaf were not only physical ones, they were signs, signs that the spiritually deaf can be made to hear, yes in today's world. But technique will not accomplish it, nor any kind of human skill, but the risen Christ and his dynamic Holy Spirit can accomplish it. The deaf can be made to hear. It astonishes us, as I was astonished only last week when I read of a candidate for the Church of England ministry, and now in

11

training, who not so very long ago was peddling drugs. But the light of Christ broke in, he heard the Word of God and responded. He in fact became a new man. He even looked different.

3

THE LIBERAL APPROACH

For he who is not against us is on our side.
MARK 9.40 (NEB)

During the last ten years or so, the word 'liberal' has become
almost a dirty word in theological circles, and not only there
but in church and Christian circles generally. This is because
it seemed to imply a weak hold on basic Christian beliefs
such as the incarnation and the resurrection, if not a partial
denial of them altogether. And being, in some degree at least,
negative, it did not build up congregations and produce
flourishing churches. This was yesterday's situation. Today
there is something like a reaction. Fundamentalism has been
on the increase. Extremes, then, are what we have witnessed,
and so it would appear that the time has come for a more
balanced approach. There needs to be a committed but open
approach to our Christian faith, that is to say at the same time
as a positive one. This is the subject of this sermon, and the
text is the saying of Jesus, 'For he who is not against us is on
our side,' the conclusion of what the New Testament scholars
would call a pronouncement story. Its liberalism all but
astonishes us. Was Jesus really open like this?

1 THE OPENNESS OF JESUS

Let us begin with the story to which this saying is the
punchline at the end. It begins with Jesus and his disciples
making a journey through the Galilean countryside. He was
avoiding the crowds and the publicity which his presence

13

invariably attracted, because he wanted to teach his disciples, and in particular to alert them to the violent end which would all too soon take place. They found what he had to say on this impossible to grasp, so contrary was it to their own thinking, but they were afraid to ask him what he meant. We can imagine an awkward silence as the group proceeded along the road, perhaps with some degree of tension. So they reached the lakeside at Capernaum and entered into a house, probably that belonging to Peter. That there was tension is evidenced by Jesus' question put to these men as soon as they were inside. 'What were you arguing about on the way?' Did they look sheepish? Anyway, they kept silent because on the road they had been discussing who was the greatest, and they knew Jesus' thoughts on this. Deliberately he sat down like the Teacher he was and, gathering the twelve disciples round him, said, 'If anyone wants to be first, he must make himself last of all and servant of all.' Then he took a child, presumably one in the house, set him in front of them, as a kind of object lesson, and putting his arm around him said, 'Whoever receives one of these children in my name [i.e., for my sake] receives me; and whoever receives me, receives not me but the One who sent me.'

Did the disciples stare at each other in open-mouthed bewilderment? That would be my guess. After all, what Jesus was saying was so liberal. No creed, no dogma, nothing to sign! Then one of the disciples spoke up. This was John, the only time in the synoptic gospels he is reported as saying anything. He was the younger brother of James, both of them noted for their forwardness in everything. They wanted to be in front and exclusively in front. This liberal approach of Jesus prompted him to recall what he had recently seen, a man operating as an exorcist on his own but using the name of Jesus. 'He wasn't one of us,' said John. That was enough. It disqualified him at once. It was the 'us and them' mentality, the 'closed shop' idea applied to Jesus and his band of twelve disciples. Outside of that there was to be no activity in Jesus' name.

Exclusiveness and protectionism setting in, and rightly so according to John's thinking then. (He moved a long way from that in due course, as St John's gospel Chapter 1 shows.) But on this occasion not only John but the other disciple with him tried to stop this freelance operator. Whether they succeeded or not we are not told, but Jesus was definite. 'Do not stop him,' he said. 'No one who does a work of divine power in my name will be able in the same breath to speak evil of me. For he who is not against us is on our side.' Did the disciples gasp at this liberality? This was *unbelievable openness*, but Jesus said it. Did he even know the exorcist John had seen was genuine? Did he know if he was honest, that he wasn't a charlatan? Apparently not, but he gave the man the benefit of the doubt and stamped on the budding exclusiveness among the disciples. Their loyalty to him was to be supreme, he was the Christ and none other, *but they were not to operate a closed shop* among his followers. 'Do not stop him,' he ordered with respect to the independent exorcist, 'for he who is not against us is on our side.' And then he capped this combination of loyalty to himself and an attitude of openness with the words he made emphatic, 'I tell you this: if anyone gives you a cup of water to drink because you are followers of the Messiah, that man assuredly will not go unrewarded.' Note the word 'anyone'. 'If *anyone* gives you a cup of water.' To be more open and general than this is impossible. And a cup of water only, how little the expenditure involved. And the motive? Simple compassion? Basic concern? Mere human kindliness? Nothing very grand here, certainly nothing theological, but – the 'but' is important – what was done was done as an expression of recognition of, and loyalty to, the Messiah, Jesus the Christ. This is the heart of the matter. Let there be theologians, there may have to be to safeguard the Messiahship of Jesus, but what counts in the beginning and at the end, the first and last resort, is the heart consciously bound to Christ. When this is firm there can be, there should be, openness, a liberal approach to all and sundry.

15

2 OUR PREDILECTION FOR BLACK AND WHITE

This is not easy. I am sure the twelve disciples did not find it easy. It is least easy, indeed it is difficult, for the young – in years, and more particularly in the faith – to be firm and at the same time to be open. The inclination is to black and white. Forgive a personal reminiscence here, but I know something about this. I had no dramatic Christian conversion, but at the age of fourteen I came quietly but sincerely to accept Jesus as the Saviour from my sins, because of what my Mother in a few sentences told me. From then on I had a faith which was simple but real, and it has never left me. It was Christ-orientated. But being young, I saw things generally in black and white, there were no half measures, all or nothing was the proper way. And, as it happened, there was an evangelical church in the town with a strongly committed evangelical ministry. To this church I was taken, and under its influence I came. It was not unintelligent, indeed it had a respect for scholarship in biblical interpretation, but it was narrow. In consequence we all looked askance at churches not of our brand. They were outsiders. We had no vestments, no candles, no ornaments, not even a cross, and those churches which had these things did not belong to us or we to them. This was stark Calvinism. I grew up, of course. I grew up quickly. I could read the Greek New Testament at the age of seventeen. And of course my subsequent studies for a degree in theology, where the method was to question every received opinion, meant I had to broaden my thinking, but it was a painful experience. This then is the point I am making. To be both firmly committed to Christ as Lord and Saviour and at the same time to be open to people who differ from us is not easily attained, especially in the first half of our lives; later on, with age, we mellow and become more charitable, but not, it is to be hoped, losing our Christian commitment.

Are there then any anchors to which for dear life we

16

should hold on? I think there are. I count five. First, that God is the creator and sustainer of the universe. Second, that God became incarnate in Jesus, whom we call Lord and Christ. Third, that he wrought an atonement for our sins on the cross. Fourth, that he rose from the dead on what we call Easter Day. Fifth, that God shows himself at work now through the operation of his Holy Spirit. Not letting go of these anchors, we can and should be open-hearted and open-minded about thoughts and ways which differ from those we call ours. We should not eschew fellowship with other church denominations. We should recognize that other religions, that is non-Christian, have elements of truth in them and are to be respected. We should listen seriously to interpretations of the Scriptures that are more critical than those which we embrace. And because it is not easy to maintain this balance of holding fast to few essentials but being open to much else, we should be very patient with those, especially the young, who can only feel safe if they are narrowly definite about all aspects of the Christian faith and the distinctive conduct that goes with it. Jesus was patient with his twelve disciples, enabling them thereby to grow into mature apostles able to minister the gospel across the world of their day.

3 LOVE: THE KEY TO OPENNESS

The key to all this is not the achievement of a subtle balancing act between liberalism and radicalism beyond the ability of most of us, if not all of us. The key is very simple, it is the love of God in our hearts, the love made known to us in Christ and demonstrated in his earthly life for us all to see if we are willing. It was not a sickly sentimentality. Jesus could rebuke, and that sharply, but he cared for people, even those whom he rebuked; all people – age, race, class, ability or lack of ability, it made no difference; he loved people, and because he did he was open to all. Love is the

17

key. God's love in our hearts. This is what makes people open. This is what makes them attractive. So let me end with the Prayer Book Collect for Quinquagesima, only changing one word, 'love' for the old word 'charity': 'O Lord, who hast taught us that all our doings without love are nothing worth: Send thy Holy Ghost, and pour into our hearts that most excellent gift of love, the very bond of peace and of all virtues, without which whosoever liveth is counted dead before thee: Grant this for thine only Son Jesus Christ's sake. Amen.'

4

DIVORCE

*What therefore God has joined together, let not man
put asunder*
MARK 10.9 (RSV)

In a collection of memorable sayings of Jesus, this one cannot
be omitted. Since its inclusion in the marriage service in the
Book of Common Prayer in 1548 it has become widely
known. It is almost part of the common stock of people's
general knowledge. And not surprisingly, for it bears on one
of the most widespread and intimate experiences of men and
women generally, marriage, and on one which perhaps more
than any other knows the meaning of deepest joy and deepest
anguish. The subject, of course, is divorce.

This is not a rare occurrence in the modern world, and
certainly not here in Britain. Until a year or two ago it was
estimated that one in three marriages ended in divorce,
now the number is nearer one in two; that is to say, every
other marriage breaks up, many of them soon after being
contracted. And the severing of the marriage takes place now
with the minimum of ceremony, almost with the maximum of
ease. And no section of society is free from this dissolution,
from royalty to ordinary men and women.

1 AN ANSWER TO A TRAP QUESTION

The community at large, so deeply acquainted as it is with
divorce, is aware that the Church frowns on it. The Roman
Catholic Church is particularly strict, the Church of England
less so but opposed, the Free Churches more liberal. This

frowning derives not from mere dislike nor simple awareness of the greater stability of marriage that used to obtain, but ultimately and essentially from the saying of Jesus, 'What therefore God has joined together, let not man put asunder.' And before we go any further in thinking about these words, let me emphasize that this saying, especially as set out in St Mark's gospel, is universally recognized by scholars as authentic. Not even the most liberal New Testament criticism has felt able to question this saying. Jesus did say this. His teaching was that marriage is a lifelong bond not to be broken. The New English Bible renders the words with the utmost clarity, 'What God has joined together, let not man separate.'

Now when did Jesus come to say this about marriage? Let me be quick to emphasize, not in a sermon or dissertation on marriage. It constitutes part of his reply to a trap question in the presence of a crowd: 'Is it lawful for a man to divorce his wife?' The trap was Deuteronomy 24 verses 1 to 4, which says it is possible, so if Jesus said no he could be charged with breaking the sacrosanct law of Moses. Surprisingly for the questioner he did not say no. He said Moses allowed divorce for people's hardness of heart. 'But from the beginning of creation God made them male and female . . . What therefore God has joined together, let not man put asunder.' Or did the questioner hope to catch Jesus in a trap with the civil authorities? Herod Antipas, the governor of Judaea had put away his wife and married another.

2 MARRIAGE AMONG THE JEWS, THE GREEKS AND THE ROMANS

This saying was indeed given by Jesus in answer to a trap question, but it was also given at a time when the whole question of marriage and divorce was a live issue, even more than it is with us today. The marriage bond in Jesus' day was in danger of disappearing altogether, especially among the

20

Greeks and the Romans. Among the Jews it is true that marriage was a high ideal and divorce was abhorred. What is more, marriage was a *duty* in order to beget children. The practice, however, fell far short of the ideal. The basic trouble was that in the eyes of the law a woman was counted as a thing. She was at the absolute disposal of her father or her husband. She had no say. A man could divorce his wife for any reason whatsoever; but not the woman, she could not divorce her husband for any reason at all. Moreover, what were regarded as legitimate reasons for a man to divorce his wife broke down into two attitudes, one very strict and the other very liberal, the latter allowing divorce if the man was simply attracted by a woman more desirable than his wife. And of course, human nature being what it is, the liberal view prevailed. So in Jesus' day, among the Jews marriage and family life was in danger of collapsing. Thus when he said, 'What therefore God has joined together, let not man put asunder,' he was not speaking in idealistic terms, but as a reformer seeking to counteract a serious situation in the community.

So much for Jewry. What about the nations outside, the Greeks and the Romans. What was the situation there? We have to concern ourselves with them because only a very short time elapsed before the Christian gospel was being proclaimed to these people. So they heard of a Jesus with these words on his lips, 'What therefore God has joined together, let not man put asunder.' And they were bidden to put their faith in him and to follow him. What could they make of this? What were they to do? It cut across their whole way of life to which they were accustomed.

Among the Greeks sexual relationships outside marriage were the ordinary and conventional thing, they carried no stigma whatsoever, but what really wrecked marriage was the low estimate of woman. The man could be as free as he liked, but from the woman the utmost moral purity was demanded. She could not even meet men, she had to live in social seclusion. The Greek married for social security in his home and reckoned to take his pleasures elsewhere. And he

21

could divorce his wife without any legal process at all. All he required was two witnesses that he had dismissed her. All this, however, was only one side of the coin. The other was the vast array of prostitutes that operated in the Greek cities. In the temple of Aphrodite in Corinth there were a thousand sacred priestesses who were available for hire when they came down into the streets in the evenings. In addition to them there was a special class of women. These were the mistresses of the famous in the community; they were cultured and lived with their men in luxurious houses. Pericles, the greatest of all Greek orators, had his women, and so did Socrates.

The situation among the Romans was different. Originally the whole of Roman religion and history was based upon the home, where the father was absolutely dominant, even to the extent of having power over life and death. And the Roman matron was not secluded like her Greek counterpart, she was prominent in all walks of life. So marriage was lifelong and prostitutes were held in contempt. For the first five hundred years of the Roman commonwealth there was not one single recorded case of divorce. Then Rome conquered Greece and the defeated conquered their victors in their way of life. By the second century Greek morale had begun to infiltrate into Roman society and soon overwhelmed it. Divorce became as common as marriage and the fashion was to go childless. So alarming was this for the future of the nation that special taxes were levied on the unmarried.

Considering, then, the parlous state of marriage in the sophisticated and pagan world outside Jewry in Jesus' time, it is a remarkable fact that the apostles and particularly St Paul dared to carry the proclamation of Jesus as the Saviour, the Jesus who said, 'What therefore God has joined together, let not man put asunder.' Of course they met opposition and ridicule, but St Paul took that message even to Corinth, where was the notorious temple of Aphrodite, and more remarkable still established a church there. In the New Testament there are two substantial letters written to the Christians in Corinth. In the first of them a whole chapter is devoted to marriage. This is amazing. The Christians in Corinth were *expected* to safeguard their marriage and not engage in divorce, the man and the woman both placed on an equal footing. It was revolutionary, but the Church grew and no stronger evidence for the power of the Christian gospel can hardly be found than in the fact that these Greeks took to Jesus as their Lord and Master, who said, 'What therefore God has joined together, let not man put asunder.'

3 CHRIST DID NOT LEGISLATE

And now let me say this with our modern church situation in mind: Christ did not legislate about marriage and divorce, what he did was to point to the ideal and to God's purpose in creating man and woman. He said, 'From the beginning of creation, God made them male and female. For this reason a man shall leave his father and mother and be joined to his wife and the two shall become one. So they are no longer two but one.' No, he did not legislate, but all who came after and called themselves Christians were expected to aspire to the ideal he clearly proclaimed. At all times, even from the earliest days of the Church's existence, there has been a temptation to make hard-and-fast regulations in this sphere. It is just possible that we can even see the beginnings of the urge in the way St Matthew wrote in Chapter 19.3–9 what Mark has in his Chapter 10.2–9. This is a subject for careful New Testament critical scholarship out of place in a sermon. This however is certain. Christians were *expected*, that is the word, expected to adhere to the Lord's saying about marriage. This ideal is the Christian standard. It still is. And because it is an ideal it is not properly subject to enforcement by rules and regulations. There will be cases where divorce is best, but it must always be undergone, where it is undergone, with regret, for it is a declension from the Lord's ideal. What is sad and serious is when Christians involved in a divorce do not recognize this.

What, however, shall we say about the non-Christian world outside the Church, especially in the so-called Christian West, where divorce has gone on and is going on apace. If the Church cannot legislate for its own members, though expecting them to eschew divorce, it certainly cannot legislate for those outside its allegiance. But this it can do and should do: point out that the community in general would be in a far happier and healthy state if it paid a proper regard to the Christian ideal in marriage. Jewry and more drastically the Greeks and Romans saw the break-up of national life when their home lives broke up through the almost total collapse of the marriage bond. All of which means that not only Christians but the man and woman in general should take seriously the saying of Jesus, 'What therefore God has joined together, let not man put asunder' (Mark 10.9).

5
THE WEALTHY

*It is easier for a camel to pass through the eye of a needle
than for a rich man to enter the kingdom of God.*
MARK 10.25 (NEB)

Jesus had many things to say about the wealthy, but this
is his most severe saying on the subject. Perhaps our first
reaction is to write it off as having no relevance to us. We are
not wealthy. I speak for myself! But if not riches, certainly
money is one of the prime interests in the modern world,
if not actually *the predominant concern* of most people.
Yesterday it was the football pools, today the National
Lottery. How to get rich quick. And every day almost every
hour we are provided with up-to-date information about the
money markets both here and abroad. And all the talk is of
inflation, a common currency, exorbitantly high salaries paid
to a privileged few, minimal wage increases for the majority,
with the growing threat of strikes for more, and over against
all this the existence of an underclass trapped in poverty.
Money, money, money! What ought to be the attitude of the
Christian towards this financial preoccupation? What did
Jesus say?

1 RICHES ARE NOT AN AUTOMATIC BAR

First I have to emphasize that Jesus was not without more
ado opposed to wealth. He did not dismiss individual rich
men and women as beyond the pale! There has to be money.
Life could not continue without it. And he himself was
indebted to some well-to-do people. St Luke provides the

names of some women who provided for Jesus and his twelve disciples (out of their own resources). And Joseph of Arimathea, described in St Matthew's gospel as 'a man of means', provided the tomb in which the body of Jesus taken down from the cross was laid. Without this the circumstantial evidence for the resurrection would be lacking. And there is the moving story of the young man who had great wealth. It is worth our attention. This young man came running up to Jesus, kneeling to him and asking, 'Good Master, what must I do to win eternal life?' When he was referred to the commandment he replied, 'But, Master, I have kept all these since I was a boy.' Now note what comes next, note it carefully. Jesus looked straight at him; his heart warmed to him, yes, a man of great wealth, and he said, 'One thing *you* lack [emphasis on you]: go, sell everything you have, and give to the poor, and you will have riches in heaven; and come, follow me.' At these words his face fell and he went away with a heavy heart. And I expect Jesus had a heavy heart to see him go. He liked this rich young man.

When he was gone Jesus looked round at his disciples. This is the second time in this short narrative we are told how Jesus used his eyes. Then he said to them, 'How hard it is for the wealthy to enter the kingdom of God!' They were amazed at this, but he insisted, 'Children, how hard it is to enter the kingdom of God! It is easier for a camel to pass through the eye of a needle than for a rich man to enter the kingdom of God.' Some commentators try to soften this statement. They say the Greek word for camel can mean rope; and the 'eye of a needle', they argue, refers to a particularly narrow gate in Jerusalem's city wall which a camel could pass through with extreme difficulty. Possibly; it is best, however, to leave the statement as it stands. What Jesus said in effect was that it is virtually impossible for a rich man to enter the kingdom of God. This astonished his disciples so much that they said one to another, 'Then who can be saved?'

As they saw the situation the rich had a far better chance of entering the kingdom of God because, for one thing, they had the time for attendance at religious festivals when the vast majority of people had to be working. They could also make munificent gifts to the Temple and earn the title of public benefactor. All in all the rich were in a privileged position for entry into the kingdom of God. When therefore Jesus said their entry was a virtual impossibility they were nonplussed. Nothing made sense. Then Jesus looked at them and said, 'For men it is impossible, but not for God; everything is possible for God.' And throughout Christian history there have been, and no doubt still are, striking examples of rich men sacrificing their wealth for a life of Christian service; some have gone to live penniless in monasteries, some have left all the comfort of Western civilization to become missionaries in what we now call the 'Third World', some have continued with their comfortable existence at home, but since their comfort was their last concern they have given themselves in sacrificial community service. No, not every wealthy man or woman professing the Christian way of life must sell all to follow Christ. Where would the Christian Church and the Christian mission in the world be without their generous giving? Their giving *is their service*. Jesus, however, looking into the face of this wealthy young man who came begging to know what he must do to enter the kingdom of God, saw that for him, yes, for him, not for everyone, there had to be separation from his riches. The pity was, as Jesus saw, he could not make the break.

2 RICHES ARE DANGEROUS

How then are we to regard wealth if we profess to be Christians – that it is essentially evil? Money is not wicked itself, but to possess it is dangerous, it may even militate against entry into the kingdom of God. Entry there depends upon the heart, not the pocket, and riches can corrupt the heart very easily. Think how readily rich people become *proud* people, how readily they look down on the poor, sometimes mocking their clothing, which after all is all they can afford. Think too how *anxious* rich people often are. As someone has said, they have spent the first half of their lives striving to amass that big bank balance and then spend the second half of their lives worrying how to keep it. Think too how self-centred rich people often become. What they want, what they enjoy, or think they do, what schemes they undertake for their own comfort. And worst of all, the rich can become *oppressors*. They can become cruel, sympathy is one of the first casualties among the very rich. If it is possible to avoid these repelling characteristics, and it is possible, then entry for the rich man into the kingdom of God is open, wide open, with the help of the grace of God. So the saying of Jesus in this connection, 'For man it is impossible, but not for God; everything is possible for God.'

But are we right to think of riches solely in money terms? There are other forms of riches. Some individuals are rich in intellectual skills. How readily, it must be said, however regretfully, they very often despise the uneducated, the people who speak with a local accent, the people whose height of musical appreciation is 'pop music', whose sun rises and sets in football. If to call such people 'snobs' is correct, then the text can be rephrased, 'How hard it will be for snobs to enter the, kingdom of God!' Why? Because the condition of entry is humility. Not what I have, not what I can do, gains entry, but the willing acceptance of the grace of God and a readiness to confess, 'Not my own merit, but by the grace of God I am what I am.'

And then there is family background. This is a form of riches. Pedigree is not to be overlooked, but it is no guarantee of distinguished living. Aristocrats have produced rakes in their families before now. The fact is, however, that men and women from 'good families', as they are often loosely called, are more likely to be noticed in the race of life, and this in itself helps them to the attainment of high positions. They have a good start, which may not lead to any particularly significant occupation or profession, but probably will. Pedigree, then, is a form of wealth. But this is the liability, and it is a real danger, inordinate pride and exclusiveness, and this is not attractive. We must however be careful to avoid sweeping judgements about pedigree, as also about the other forms of wealth. It is worth noting that the story of Jesus, indeed the New Testament itself, begins with his pedigree. No doubt we find this a boring introduction and probably skip it, but not his contemporaries. They were avid to find out that he came from the royal line of David, for the Messiah was held to be descended from him. But he did not trade on this in any way, he was 'meek and lowly in heart', in whose presence even the humblest were at ease. Is this a lesson for those who are nobly born?

Money, individual skills, a distinguished pedigree, these are some of the riches that some people possess. They are not in themselves bad, but they are dangerous. This is why Jesus said, 'How hard it will be for the wealthy to enter the kingdom of God!' or even more strongly, 'It is easier or a camel to pass through the eye of a needle than for a rich man to enter the kingdom of God!' And the reason is that entry into the kingdom of God requires of necessity humility. We have to stoop to go through the gate, perhaps even crawl! Reliance on our possessions of whatever kind will not avail, though we may be very conscious of them and rightly so.

3 THE KINGDOM OF GOD

But what is the kingdom of God? Is it a glorious future beyond the grave? Yes it is, and the twelve disciples of Jesus had their eyes on this and expected to be privileged to sit on the throne there. Jesus did not exclude this interpretation, though he was quick to point out that the first shall be last and the last first. What he emphasized, however, was the kingdom of God as a present experience now in this life. It is doing the will of God, and that is not easy for any of us, for by nature we long to go our own way, but it is especially difficult for the wealthy who reckon they have the means to do so, and that with satisfaction. But Jesus said, 'How hard it will be for the wealthy to enter the kingdom of God! It is even easier for a camel to pass through the eye of a needle . . . !'

One person who understood this was Mary the mother of Jesus. It was an awareness which has come down to us in the pages of St Luke's gospel in what has come to be called the Magnificat:

> Tell out, my soul, the greatness of the Lord,
> rejoice, rejoice, my spirit, in God my saviour;
> so tenderly has he looked upon his servant, humble
>   as she is . . .
> The arrogant of heart and mind he has put to rout,
> he has torn imperial powers from their thrones,
>   but the humble have been lifted high.
> The hungry he has satisfied with good things,
>   the rich sent empty away . . .
>   (Luke 1.46–48, 51–53)

Come back to the text, the distinguished saying of Jesus addressed to his disciples, 'It is easier for a camel to pass through the eye of a needle than for a rich man to enter the kingdom of God.' To which he added this after comment, 'For men it is impossible, but not for God; everything is possible for God.' There are some glorious examples of this in Christian history. One of the earliest, perhaps the earliest, is the story of Levi in the gospel (Luke 5.27–32). He was a tax-gatherer and was therefore rich. The only rich classes in Jesus' time were the tax-gatherers and the Sadducees. But Levi made the break, he became a disciple. Truly for God everything is possible. Wealthy people are and will be in the kingdom of God. Of that we can be certain.

6

CONCERNING AMBITION

Whoever wants to be great must be your servant.
MARK 10.43 (NEB)

These distinctive and memorable sayings of Jesus were not part of a lecture or some theological discourse of his. Perhaps it is too much to claim that they were 'off the cuff' remarks, but certainly they arose out of concrete situations and events and were a response to them. This is true of the saying in St Mark 10.43 and paralleled in St Matthew 20.25–26, 'Whoever wants to be great must be your servant, and whoever wants to be first must be the willing slave of all.' Clearly the matter in mind here is ambition. It arose because two of his disciples and their mother approached him for a favour. They were quite open about it, 'Master, we should like you to do us a favour.' (St Matthew in his account says, 'The mother of Zebedee's sons *then* came before him, with her sons. She bowed low and begged a favour.') 'What is it you wish?' asked Jesus. They answered, 'Grant us the right to sit in state with you, one at your right and the other at your left.' So the sons were involved with the mother. Perhaps it was they who begged her to speak up on their behalf.

Well, well, well. I hesitate to use the word 'cheek', but it can hardly stop coming to mind. Who were these people? The mother, I want to say 'pushing' mother, if her name was Salome, and this is the general opinion, then she was the sister of Mary the mother of Jesus. Would it be a wild guess, then, to suggest that as part of the family 'so to speak' she thought she had a right to ask for favours, not least on behalf of her two sons James and John, if not for herself?

31

Furthermore, Zebedee, the father, was a well-to-do fisher-man on the lake of Galilee and probably lived in Capernaum. They kept servants and so, it may be, counted themselves as superior in the community by the lake. The family had done well and hoped, even expected, to do better. We shall not be far wrong, therefore, if we label them as *ambitious* people. About Zebedee we don't know, he drops out of the story entirely, but mother and sons put themselves to the fore. They were ambitious.

1 SIDELIGHT ON AMBITION

Before we look more deeply into the incident, I feel bound to say that they chose a most inopportune time to come with their request. Jesus was on the road going up to Jerusalem, he leading the way. The disciples were filled with awe and those who followed behind were afraid. Jesus then took the Twelve aside and began to tell them what was to happen to him. 'We are now going to Jerusalem,' he said, 'and the Son of Man will be given up to the chief priests and the doctors of the law; they will condemn him to death and hand him over to the foreign power . . . ' The mother of Zebedee's sons then came (notice that 'then came') before him with her sons. She bowed and begged a favour. What unbelievable insensitivity! The time and the occasion could scarcely be more inappropriate. But Matthew's account is explicit as to the occasion, thereby telling us one terrible truth about ambition, whosoever has it, it can be unbelievably *insensitive*, so wrapped up is it in its own concerns and wishes. The phrase 'blind ambition' springs to mind. But is ambition a bad thing? Here are some parents sadly reading their son's school report. No, it wasn't a disastrous report. The boy wasn't bottom in every examination and he wasn't trouble-some, but the headmaster had this to say, 'I'm afraid he won't do very well at anything, he is quite happy to scrape along at the bottom, just avoiding failure, he seems to have no ambition!' From which we may gather that ambition, far from being a bad thing, is a good characteristic; even a necessary one for modest success in life. But ambition can be dangerous. In this it is like wealth, indeed it is a form of wealth, it needs to be kept under control or it will lead to most unfortunate consequences, if not disasters.

It does not seem that James and John kept their ambition under control in the early days of their discipleship of Jesus. When Jesus was making his last journey to Jerusalem, knowing that crucifixion awaited him, he sent messengers ahead to prepare the way. When they entered a Samaritan village, however, the villagers refused them either a lodging or even a passage through for no other reason than they were on their way to Jerusalem, so bitter was the hostility between Jews and the Samaritans. The reaction of James and John was swift and bitter. They seemed to have learned nothing of their Master's spirit. They said to him, 'Lord, may we call down fire from heaven to burn them up?' Yes, burn them up! For that they earned a rebuke from Jesus and had quietly to proceed to another village. No wonder he had nicknamed the brothers 'Boanerges, Sons of Thunder'. They were *impulsive*, impatient young men, ready for violence if necessary, ready to fight their way through in life to gain their objective. In them we see ambition at its most crude.

Properly understood, ambition is raw material needing to be processed to be of value. And it was checked by Jesus directly after they came asking for a favour from him. 'Grant us to sit in state with you, one at your right and the other at your left.' The RSV has 'in your glory'. They were told they did not understand what they were asking. So *ignorance* was added to the other unfortunate consequences of their ambition. But they were not conscious of it, so full were they of their own importance. 'Can you drink the cup that I drink or be baptized with the baptism that I am baptized?' Proudly they answered, 'We can.' Their own ambition knew no bounds. Then he puzzled them. 'The cup that I drink you shall drink, and the baptism I am baptized with shall be your

33

baptism; but to sit at my right or left is not for me to grant; it is for those to whom it has already been assigned.' Then the other ten disciples (who apparently were not present when this was said) were indignant with James and John, these 'cocky', ambitious young men! But Jesus called them to him and said, 'You know that in the world the recognized rulers lord it over their subjects, and their great men make them feel the weight of authority. That is not the way with you; among you, whoever wants to be great must be your servant, and whoever wants to be first must be the willing slave of all. For even the Son of Man did not come to be served but to serve, and to surrender his life as a ransom for many.'

And then the shock for James and John. Only a matter of days later they were with Peter in what is called the agony in the garden, Gethsemane, and only a few hours later he was nailed to that horrible cross; but *that was his coming in glory*, there he was sacrificing himself for our redemption, and there were two men present with him, one on his right and one on his left, sharing with him the same agonizing death. Both of them malefactors, that is criminals. And to think that they, James and John, with their mother, had asked the favour of occupying those two places, not knowing what they were asking! They must have wished when they saw those three crosses that they had torn their ambitious tongues out of their mouths. Their ambition had all but made fools of them.

2 JESUS CHOSE THESE AMBITIOUS MEN

But Jesus wanted these two boisterous, energetic young men to be his disciples, their ambition notwithstanding. They would have to learn, however. So it was these two (with Peter, who was a different kind of man), not the rest of the Twelve, who were given the privilege of seeing the raising of Jairus's daughter to life and of ascending with Jesus up what is called the Mount of Transfiguration and witnessing his glory. The other nine disciples saw none of this. All of which cries aloud that ambition does not automatically disqualify for a privileged position in the kingdom of God, *but it has to be disciplined first*. These two, James and John, did acquire stature, though their ambition was not realized in the way they thought. James being the first of the twelve apostles to suffer a martyr's death, he did indeed drink the cup of which Jesus spoke. In AD 44 Herod Agrippa killed James the brother of John with a sword. No more summary of his death was possible. It is dismissed with the minimum of words in Acts Chapter 12. But he won a martyr's crown, and there is no brighter crown in the service of Jesus, Lord and Master. There his ambition rested.

3 WHEN AMBITION IS SAFE

Ambition is only safe when it is directed towards a task or for the benefit of other people, not – and this is the crux of the matter – when it is centred on itself. It is not wrong to strive to excel at some skill, playing a musical instrument, designing attractive and serviceable buildings, becoming an expert in surgery, but it is dangerous if the aim in any of these pursuits is to build up the *ego*. What is even better than their skills, and others like them, is if the aim is to benefit other people, individuals, the community, disadvantaged people. Jesus turned the spotlight on this when he spoke of the way recognized rulers in the world made people feel the weight of their authority. He expected his disciples to be different. 'This is not the way with you,' he said, 'among you, whoever wants to be great must be your servant, and whoever wants to be first must be the willing slave of all.' So he stood the general notion about ambition on its head. The Christian's ambition must be to serve people, not to dominate them and not to make them feel inadequate. *In this way* Jesus himself strove to be first, not to be ministered unto but to go all the way in service and to surrender his life as a ransom for many.

35

There is a lesson here for all of us who are Christian people, but to none more pointedly than for priests. Priests can be ambitious. In their early years they can have an eye on promotion and can bend their energies to this end. They are ready to 'trim their sails' and to compromise such principles as they have in order to mount the right band-wagon (as they see it). They long for publicity and to be 'in the news'. And some succeed. There are proud prelates and there are evangelists proud to have achieved their ambition in drawing vast crowds. Pity they haven't learned the lesson about ambition from James and John and what Jesus said to them, 'Among you, whoever wants to be great must be your servant, and whoever wants to be first must be the willing slave of all.'

But don't miss the fact that Jesus wanted James and John, those two ambitious men, to be his disciples. It is not wrong to be ambitious, but it needs spiritual surgery to make it Christian and serviceable. And don't forget, James and John became leading apostles because they were specially loved by Jesus, warts and all.

7
IMAGINATIVE PRAYER

I tell you, then, whatever you ask for in prayer, believe that
you have received it and it will be yours.
MARK 11.24 (NEB)

I have chosen to preach on this saying of Jesus, not because
it is luminous, but for the opposite reason, because it is
puzzling; indeed, as it stands it hardly makes sense. It also
stands as an illustration of what I have tried to point out with
respect to some other sayings of Jesus, that we cannot plumb
the meaning of them unless we are prepared to study them
in relation to their context. Or to put the matter another way,
unless we are prepared to study when Jesus said what he did
and why. Some light is then thrown on the saying itself.

1 THE CRISIS WEEK

Now the saying from Mark 11.24 was uttered by Jesus on
the Tuesday morning before the Friday we call Good Friday,
when he was crucified. It was Jesus' crisis week. It was also
crisis week for the Jewish nation. Jesus as the Christ had
reached the climax of his ministry, and the nation had
reached the climax of its existence as a settled people. It was
a time of breaking up, a time of epoch-making proportions.
Nothing was the same after this week.

It began with what we call the triumphal entry of Jesus into
Jerusalem on Palm Sunday. The day was momentous
because unlike his unerring custom hitherto, he openly
and publicly accepted the acclamation of the crowds:
'Hosanna! Blessings on him who comes in the name of the

Lord! Blessings on the coming kingdom of our father David! Hosanna in the heavens!' The shouting represented the noisy longing of the nation for a restoration of its ancient sovereignty and independence. It was a nationalistic demonstration.

Jesus saw the situation in an entirely different light. When he reached the city he entered the Temple and looked around. It was a tour of inspection. What he saw saddened him. Far from being the spiritual powerhouse for the nation it was meant to be, it had degenerated into a money-making racket. And that, said Jesus, signalled the nation's ultimate break-up as a sovereign people. We can of course distance ourselves from this. It is ancient history. It relates to one particular people at one particular time. But there is a message, indeed a warning for every nation and our nation. When spiritual values are counted of no consequence and market forces, science and politics are reckoned sufficient to elevate a people, decline is bound to set in. Dr Sacks, the Chief Rabbi in England, a remarkable man, has pointed this out in his recently published book entitled *Faith in the Future*. We need to learn our lesson. Jerusalem did not learn hers. Christ was crucified. He was an embarrassment. The spiritual was openly rejected.

2 OBSTRUCTING MOUNTAINS

On the Monday following the tour of inspection of the Temple which Jesus conducted on the Sunday, he returned to the city, and being hungry approached a fig tree he saw in full leaf, in the hope of finding figs, but there were none. He addressed the tree thus, 'May no one ever again eat fruit from you!' His disciples listened. Next day, passing the tree again, they observed that it had withered from the roots up. Peter drew the attention of Jesus to it, and this was his comment, 'Have faith in God. I tell you this: if anyone says to this mountain, "Be lifted from your place and hurled into

38

the sea", and has no inward doubts, but believes that what he says is happening, it will be done for him. I tell you, then, whatever you ask for in prayer, believe that you have received it and it will be yours.'

First we must note the repeated 'I tell you'. Whenever Jesus prefixed his sayings with this introduction – and there are some five or six cases in the gospels – he was marking out what he had to say as of particular importance. Here he speaks of lifting up a mountain and hurling it into the sea. No one could ever imagine that he meant this literally. Obviously it is a metaphor for a difficulty or obstacle judged, and rightly judged, to be beyond the possibility of removal, but not beyond the power of God. This is the point. Prayer in faith puts us in touch with that power. Not casual, perfunctory prayer, not the mere mechanical recital of liturgical phrases, but such imaginative prayer as is able actually to visualize what is asked for happening. This is the lively faith required. Half-hearted prayer accomplishes nothing. There must be no secret thinking such as 'Well, I'll try praying about my problem, it might work, it might accomplish something.' God does not respond to that kind of prayer. There is no chance of God removing the mountain of difficulty that blocks our progress unless we firmly believe God can accomplish what seems impossible; yes, accomplish it for us, if it is his will.

3 THE OBSTRUCTING MOUNTAIN FOR THE JEWISH NATION

What was the mountain blocking the path of the Jewish people towards spiritual stature and leadership in Jesus' day? It was the preoccupation with money, mercantile success and comfort, the symptoms of which Jesus saw when he paid that inspection tour of the Temple on what we call Palm Sunday; it was the almost complete absence of spirituality and the dominance of worldliness. How could the nation ever rise to a position of leadership for the welfare of the people? It was inconceivable, but it had actually happened before in Israel's long history. It could be imagined as happening again, imagined when shot through with the prayer of faith in the power of God. It sounds so simple. So did Jesus' action on that Monday morning when he said to the barren fig tree, 'May no one ever again eat fruit from you!' Next day the disciples saw it had withered. What astonished them was the simplicity of Jesus' action. He only spoke to the tree. What impressed them was the power of Jesus' word. He had that power because he was in touch with the power of God; it was God's power, brought into action through Jesus' confident imagination that what he asked would take place. 'I tell you, then,' said Jesus to his open-mouthed and open-eyed disciples, 'whatever you ask for in prayer, believe that you have received it and it will be yours.'

Was the mountain of Israel's intransigence and worldliness removed and hurled into the sea? Did the robbers' cave, as Jesus called the Temple, come to be of no account as far as spirituality was concerned? The answer is yes. But, and this is the wonder, this is the miracle, there was born a new spirituality, born out of the evil deed called the crucifixion of Jesus. There came to be a powerful gospel of the cross of Christ which broke through national barriers and frontiers, bearing a message of hope, broad and strong, for all people ready to forgive and ready to love. Did this seem even remotely possible when Jesus entered the Jerusalem Temple on Palm Sunday, as we call it? But it happened, and the Christian gospel has been around and across the world.

4 AN APPEAL

Nothing is too hard for God, not even removing a mountain of difficulty, not even quickening a whole people or an individual person trapped in worldliness and wickedness. We must never limit the power of God. We must never

40

circumscribe the possibilities open to us and people we know in the light of the power of God. We must actually believe in God and we must pray in imaginative faith.

It may be that I am unknowingly addressing someone undergoing severe trouble at the present time and beset with problems of lesser or greater magnitude. My friend, do not give up, do not write off your situation as hopeless. Do not despair of that person you know with a severe illness. God can remove mountains, and the outcome of praying in imaginative faith is very often a miracle.

My text for the sermon, 'I tell you, then, whatever you ask for in prayer, believe that you have received it and it will be yours,' could be described as the last *general* saying of Jesus recorded in the synoptic gospels. What amazes me is when he said it. Everything and almost everybody was against him. The Pharisees, the Sadducees, the Herodians, the common people, even they went to Calvary to watch his crucifixion. Yet he remained unruffled, free from fear, free from anxiety, unbelievably calm. He believed in the power of God. He prayed that God would remove the cup of suffering from him, and when he did not, he still trusted. Jesus is not only our teacher on whose lips were striking sayings, he is also our example. May we seek the grace of God and walk in his steps.

8

OUR TWO DEBTS

Pay Caesar what is due to Caesar, and pay God what is due to God.

MARK 12.17 (NEB)

This is one of the most famous of Jesus' sayings, and one that has had important consequences, not least for governments, in the way it is interpreted. In the first instance it is concerned with the payment of taxes to the civil authority and is not likely to be of minimal interest to the majority of people. No one likes paying taxes. What had Jesus to say on this?

1 THE OCCASION FOR THIS SAYING

First we must look at the context of the saying. When did Jesus say this and why? The time was towards the close of his ministry, and the place Jerusalem. The scribes and Pharisees and the chief priests were growing desperate. Try what devices they might, they failed to catch him. Their aim was to ensnare him with the ruling authorities so that they, the Romans, would arrest him. But Jesus was not easy to ensnare, he was a match for them. One day, however, they thought they were on a winning scheme. A group of harmless-looking and plausible Pharisees were sent, probably by the Sanhedrin, to execute their 'coup'. They took with them some men of Herod's party who were not in sympathy with the Pharisees. The idea was to hide their hostility. So they approached Jesus blandly and with flattery. 'Master, you are an honest man, we know, and truckle to no one, whoever he

42

may be; you teach in all honesty the way of life that God requires.' This was 'laying it on thick'. Then came the trap question which they reckoned would make him fall foul of the civil authorities. This was the question, 'Are we or are we not permitted to pay taxes to the Roman Emperor?' They wanted a straight answer to a straight question. So they rephrased it in the bluntest possible words, 'Shall we pay or not?' Full of suspense, they waited for his reply. Did he keep them waiting? He saw how crafty their question was. 'Why are you trying to catch me out?' he asked. 'Fetch me a silver piece, and let me look at it.' Clearly neither Jesus nor his questioners had the hated Roman coin upon them with which the taxes had to be paid. Someone was dispatched to fetch a coin. This must have taken a little time. Holding it up, Jesus asked, 'Whose head is this; and whose inscription?' 'Caesar's', they replied. They could not give any other answer. Then Jesus said, 'Pay Caesar what is due to Caesar, and pay God what is due to God.' They heard him with astonishment. They never expected this answer. Their trap was a failure.

Before we consider what Jesus meant by this saying, we ought to turn aside for a moment to see what these taxes were that Jews in Palestine had to pay in Jesus' time. There was the Jewish tax which Jews subscribed to for the upkeep of the Temple and the cost of the ceremonial sacrifices. The shekel was the coinage used for this. It bore the head of no civil ruler. In addition there was the Roman tax imposed since the occupation of the country. It consisted of a tax on land, on property, and a poll tax all were liable to pay except the very young and the very old. The proceeds went into the Roman emperor's coffers. In Jesus' time this was Tiberius, not an honourable character to put it mildly. It had to be paid with the Roman coinage, the denarius, which bore the image of the Caesar or Emperor. So hated was it, the Jews would not carry it on their persons. The Pharisees and Herodians bent on catching Jesus in a trap felt confident that, true Jew that he was, he would refuse to pay this Roman tax. He certainly carried no denarius on his person, nor did his disciples. But no, he said, 'Pay Caesar what is due to Caesar, and pay God what is due to God.' *Exeunt* Pharisees.

2 SUBMISSION TO THE STATE

What then is the implication for Christians and for the Church in its relationship to the state, including the non-Godfearing state? In a word it is submission. In his letter to the Christians in Rome St Paul set out the matter categorically.

> Every person must submit to the supreme authorities. There is no authority but by act of God, and the existing authorities are instituted by him; consequently anyone who rebels against authority is resisting a divine institution, and those who so resist have themselves to thank for the punishment they will receive . . . That is also why you pay taxes. The authorities are in God's service and to these duties they devote their energies.
>
> (Rom 13.1–2, 6, NEB)

Submission, then, is the proper Christian attitude to the state; and for this reason it is a divine ordinance whose purpose is to maintain law and order without which chaos reigns, and if chaos reigns no life worthy of the name is possible. St Paul could not help but be aware of the benefit the Roman government provided. The peace it maintained throughout its empire enabled the Christian gospel to spread throughout its length and breadth. The *Pax Romana* was a benediction, and it was established and protected by the Roman government, indeed it existed by the will of God. This is the basic reason why Christians should submit to it. Rebellion is therefore out.

What, however, should Christians do if and when the state turns and persecutes them? This was not the situation when

44

St Paul wrote the words I have quoted from Romans Chapter 13. Even under the Emperor Nero they were left in peace along with the whole empire for five years. But then the storm broke. The Christians were dubbed (falsely, of course) as enemies of the state. Even so, at this time this is what St Peter wrote to 'God's scattered people' as he called them in his letter labelled 1 Peter in the New Testament:

> Submit yourselves to every human institution for the sake of the Lord, whether to the sovereign as supreme, or to the governor as his deputy for the punishment of criminals and the commendation of those who do right. For it is the will of God that by your good conduct you should put ignorance and stupidity to silence.

> (1 Pet 2.13–15, NEB)

This pacific and co-operative submission to the state is not unacceptable in normal circumstances, when we can believe that it exists by the will of God, but what if the state puts itself in the place of God? Should Christians submit then? This was not a situation either St Paul or St Peter faced, but such was the background of the last book of the New Testament, the Revelation or Apocalypse. Not surprisingly there is nothing about submission here, but also nothing about rebellion; on the contrary, a great deal about suffering for the faith's sake, and that in the hope of eternal life in the world to come.

So the message for Christians in relation to the state is clear. It is to submit. Rebellion is out. But there is more to be said. If the state exists by the will of God and is his instrument for the good of his world, should there not be *more than* passive obedience, should there not be active co-operation where possible? This co-operation, it must be admitted, becomes more of a practical possibility where there is a Church–state relationship, as in Britain. And here I feel bound to express my own conviction that Christians ought to be wary about seeking to untie the knot by disestablishment, in spite of the anomalies establishment brings about. Leaving that aside, a wholly beneficial situation exists when Christian men and women with the necessary skills take a practical part in state government and are seen to take part. More than that, it is to be applauded when churchmen take part in local government including borough and town councils. All this seems a long way from the time and setting of the original saying of Jesus, 'Pay Caesar what is due to Caesar, and pay God what is due to God.' But this is no small part of the reason why these sayings have survived and continue to hold the attention. There is a depth and relevance about them which makes them come alive in age after age and situation after situation, so that they drive us to conclude that they deal with eternal truth.

3 A FALSE DICHOTOMY

Now when the Pharisees put their trap question to Jesus about paying taxes to Caesar, he did not answer by merely saying they should pay, he added, 'and pay God what is due to God'. So there are two sets of obligations.

There have been attempts to keep these two obligations separate. It has been argued that there are two distinct and separate spheres in the business of living. There is our secular life and there is our religious life. It has to be said that in our time this dichotomy has led to disastrous results. In Germany, for instance, there was a period when it was held that the religious life had principles of behaviour and operation that were appropriate to it, and they were not to be confused with those that applied in the secular. And so harsh, indeed brutal, action which was frowned upon in the Christian sphere was said to be appropriate to the secular sphere, not least in the military. This is how it came about that good Christian Germans could tolerate, even justify, ruthless aggression in the name of the state. They turned to the saying of Jesus, 'Pay Caesar what is due to Caesar, and pay God what is due to God.' So they filled their churches *and* polished their weapons. But this is a false dichotomy.

The two spheres are related and act upon each other, and this makes for wholesomeness.

What then is due to Caesar and should be paid? The answer is taxes, in order that the state may have the wherewithal to operate and structure the communal life so that it does not disintegrate in chaos, to nobody's benefit. But what is due to God and should be paid? The answer is worship; it is also true that in default of this in a nation it likewise is liable to disintegrate. The story of Russia in the twentieth century is evidence. It is here that the Churches have a vital (the word is used advisedly) function to perform. They exist for worship. Let there be then impressive Houses of Parliament, but if there is no impressive cathedral in the city the communal situation is unsafe. 'Pay Caesar what is due to Caesar, and pay God what is due to God.' The application is not only to cathedrals. Churches, humble churches, local churches, should also be places of distinction, architecturally if possible, and perhaps with a peal of bells. These things are not luxuries, they are necessities for communal welfare. And what goes on in the churches should in the first place be worship and feel like worship. This has to take priority even over evangelism. The Church must be a place where this word of God can be realized, 'Be still, and know that I am God.'

So this saying of Jesus has a clear and straightforward message for all of us who profess to be Christians. We must pay our dues to the state ungrudgingly, and we must set aside some of our time (as valuable as our money) for worship of God. Only so shall we be safe.

47

9

THE RESURRECTION OF THE DEAD

God is not God of the dead but of the living.
MARK 12.27 (NEB)

I begin with a question: Ought we to support a common currency in Europe or should we not? And another question: Ought there to be devolution for Scotland or not? No, I am not going into the ins and outs of these current issues, so you can breathe a sigh of relief. In any case a sermon is not the place for such. I want to make the point that those who engage in these disputes, not least in the House of Commons, can argue their case either by careful analysis of the situation and what is involved – though it may be a lengthy and often laborious process – *or* they can adopt a different way altogether: short, sharp and very often clever and devastating, it is to make the opponents' standpoint appear ridiculous.

Now the dispute in Jesus' day, and it still exists, is concerned with the resurrection of the dead. Shall we rise or shall we not rise; indeed, when we are dead are we 'done for' or not? What is the answer, and how is the question to be answered?

1 THE PHARISEES AND THE SADDUCEES

The two main religious parties were divided on this issue. The opposing party, that is the party that denied any resurrection altogether were the Sadducees. Where they obtained this name no one seems to know, though guesses are made.

48

For the most part they belonged to aristocratic families, and from them the high priests were selected. They were priests and belonged to the Sanhedrin, the supreme governing body in the nation, though their concern was rather more with the political settlement of the country and its security than with religion. They were bitterly opposed to Jesus because they feared he might unsettle the delicate situation of the Jewish nation under the Roman occupation. They wanted him removed, but the problem was how to do so without an uproar of the people, on which the Romans would stamp at once.

Over against the Sadducees were the Pharisees. Neither party was enamoured of the other, but they had to consort with each other. The Pharisees were not wealthy like the Sadducees, but they were religious in a way the Sadducees were not. They kept the letter of the Jewish law, especially the ceremonial, and laid great stress on sabbath observance, but they were adept at keeping up appearances while bending the law to suit their convenience. They hated Jesus because he exposed their hypocrisy. Religiously, they were superior to the Sadducees and believed in the resurrection of the dead, in spirits and in angels.

2 THE SADDUCEES' TRAP QUESTION

During the last week of Jesus' ministry, as it turned out to be, both these groups, the Sadducees and the Pharisees, made deliberate attempts to embroil him in argument. First came the Pharisees, raising the hated question of payment of taxes to the Roman emperor; then came the Sadducees, hoping to make a fool of him over belief in the resurrection. They did not choose the direct method of careful debate, but instead sought to destroy Jesus in the popular esteem by making the belief appear ridiculous. 'Master,' they began, 'Moses laid it down for us that if there are brothers, and one dies leaving a wife but no child, then the next should marry

49

the widow and carry on his brother's family.' This reverent appeal to the law of Moses sounded well. They went on with their story, carefully laying the trap. 'Now there were seven brothers. The first took a wife and died without issue. Then the second married her, and he too died without issue. So did the third. Eventually the seven of them died, all without issue. Finally the woman died.' Was the conclusion meant to demolish Jesus? 'At the resurrection, when they come back to life' – what straight faces the Sadducees must have kept, for they did not believe a word of this – 'whose wife will she be, since all seven had married her?'

Jesus answered as coolly as his questioners. Today we would say, 'They did not get him rattled.' From their standpoint this was ominous. Their plan to make him appear ridiculous looked like miscarrying. 'You are mistaken,' he said, 'and surely this is the reason: you do not know either the scriptures or the power of God. When they rise from the dead, men and women do not marry; they are like angels in heaven.' He did not say sexual differentiation is non-existent in heaven, but sex is not the means of continuing existence in heaven; and he did not say the raised from the dead *become* angels, they are 'like angels in heaven'. So there are angels in heaven! Jesus believed this. All this was sober statement. But he had more to say. 'But about the resurrection of the dead, have you never read in the Book of Moses?' – he would not let these Sadducees off the hook of the Pentateuch which they counted as the basis of the religious profession, indeed it was the important plank in their public stance – 'have you never read . . . the story of the burning bush, how God spoke to him and said, "I am the God of Abraham, the God of Isaac, and the God of Jacob"?' But these patriarchs were all dead long ago! Yet God said, 'I *am* the God of those men' – not I was, I am. And then the saying which is the text of this sermon, 'God is not God of the dead but of the living.' And then, oh so politely, 'You are greatly mistaken.'

3 GOD'S LIVING RELATIONSHIP WITH THE DEPARTED

What then does this saying mean – 'God is not God of the dead but of the living'? It means that a proper basis of belief in the resurrection of the dead is not the intrinsic immortality of the soul but a living relation with God. In this passage of scripture (Exod 3.6), God shows himself as being in a vital relationship with men long since dead. The living God cannot however be in a relationship with people who no longer exist. Therefore those patriarchs, Abraham, Isaac and Jacob, were still living at the time of exodus, though not alive in this visible world, but alive to God. It is true, of course, that this does not take us beyond a belief in the immortality of the soul, it does not carry on to the resurrection of the body, but this does follow when we understand that the body is a true part of our human nature. We are to no small degree what we are because of our bodies. Without our bodies we would not have a recognizable identity. We cannot believe, therefore, that God who maintained a relationship with the departed would leave them forever without bodies. The death of the body is therefore a suspension of life as we know it in this world until some other form is granted. None of this is set out in the Old Testament. For the Hebrew people, for the most part, the afterlife was a vague shadow-like form of existence in a semi-dark underworld called Sheol. Jesus, however, in this saying, 'God is not God of the dead but of the living,' begins to open the door to a far brighter future with which the old has no comparison. And the New Testament is definite on this. Our resurrection body will not be this present body, but a new body adequate for the resurrection life but not wholly remote from the body we have now.

This saying of Jesus about the resurrection of the dead is admittedly but a tiny twinkling light. It was something. It gave comfort. It gave hope. But how different was the flood of light brought about by the actual resurrection of the crucified Jesus from his grave. But the truth of the saying of Jesus we have been considering is not rubbed away. God is in a living relationship with those who have died, men and women; they are therefore alive, though not in the visible world. 'God is not God of the dead but of the living.' More than that, they are like angels in heaven. Jesus said so.

Those who have been bereaved will hear these words as those who have not become acquainted with this grief are as yet unable. Of course these words are puzzling, but if we knew more we should be baffled more, for we cannot begin to visualize what life is like beyond our mortality. We should nevertheless hold on to the words and be at peace in our minds for those we love who are no longer with us. They are alive, alive unto God. 'For God is not God of the dead but of the living.' And they are as the angels in heaven. How wonderful! I confess I have found comfort here.

*   *   *

O you poor Sadducees, you reckoned you were on to a winner when you came to Jesus with your denial of the resurrection of the dead. You thought you could defeat him by ridicule and so brought up this story (a cock-and-bull yarn?) about a woman with seven husbands. But who was made to look stupid? Were they? Or was it Jesus? What they could never have even guessed was the consolation that their action caused to be drawn from the lips of Jesus about the dead. 'God is not God of the dead but of the living.' Perhaps we can even be grateful that the proud and stupid Sadducees told their silly story. It caused a light to shine upon what is dark for many people, our resurrection following death and the death of those whom we love. So treasure the saying!

10
LOVE YOUR ENEMIES

Love your enemies and pray for those who persecute you.
MATTHEW 5:44 (RSV)

In any selection of the sayings of Jesus to be found in the gospel narratives in the New Testament this one is 'a must', it has to be included. Along with other sayings it is clearly labelled with the prefix, 'But I say to you . . . ' So there can be no doubt, here we are given the authentic teaching of Jesus *in his own words*. What is more, it arouses immediate attention because it goes against the grain of accepted behaviour, and for those who first heard it from the lips of Jesus against the grain of the generally received wisdom. 'You have heard that it was said . . . but I say to you . . . ' Here is Jesus speaking on his own authority, speaking as an authoritative teacher. 'Never mind what has been said in the past, this is what I am telling you.' And my guess is that if we could see the reaction of his hearers we would see and perhaps hear every sign of incredulity. Impossible! Nonsense! Ridiculous. We can't sit down under this.

A second reason for choosing to turn our attention to this particular saying of Jesus is that it is one with which almost everyone is vaguely familiar who knows anything at all about the Christian religion, even people who rarely 'darken the doors' of a church. 'Love your enemies.' It is regarded as expressing the essence of Christianity in action, even though it is commonly regarded as an impossible ideal casting a shadow over the practicality of the Christian way of life altogether.

53

1 JEALOUSY MAKES ENEMIES

Perhaps we ought to note at the outset that the saying is anything but idealistic. It has the real world firmly in mind. 'Love your enemies', it says, taking for granted that *we all have enemies*. Occasionally we read, perhaps in an obituary notice, 'He hadn't an enemy in the world.' I don't believe it. There is no one without enemies. Jesus had enemies. The fact is, be a man, be a woman, as good as he, which is impossible, he/she will still have enemies. Not in the sense of armed opponents out to destroy, even to kill by physical force, but people bent on causing injury by much more subtle methods. Jealousy is often at the root of this hostility. Here is a boy at school. He does well in his examinations, sometimes he is top of the class. And out in the world later on he succeeds in his work, he marries a beautiful and able woman, he has a fine house in an attractive suburb within easy reach of London, his name is frequently in the newspapers. This is not imaginary. I have more than one real person in mind. Then jealousy gets to work, jealousy on the part of those who knew him in the early days when they were all struggling together, but this one surpassed them. And he surpassed them in public esteem, it has to be admitted not least because of his good looks, easy manner and engaging voice. So his former contemporaries came to be jealous of him, they could have done as well as he, indeed they had more accomplishments, that was the trouble. Unfortunately they came to the attitude of 'taking it out of him', as the saying goes; in a subtle way they became his enemies, losing no opportunity to snub him in public and to tarnish his reputation in private.

This is a situation that does not only obtain with men and in professional and business circles. Women also can become party to it. Too often it has its roots in dress, physical attraction, voice and manner. And if such women come to enjoy a successful marriage and worse still from this point of view a so-called brilliant marriage, they are likely to acquire enemies. There can be bitter hostilities. I have seen it happen, and the upper classes (so-called) are not free of it. I am making a point of stressing these personal hostilities that spring from jealousy because I want to make sure of bringing this saying of Jesus about loving our enemies into connection with our personal lives, where we can do something about it, and not relegate it to international situations when armed conflict is the outcome and where most of us have little influence that we can bring to bear. That way this basic saying of Jesus, 'Love your enemies', gets relegated to the wastepaper basket.

2 THE MEANING OF LOVE

And now this word love – 'Love your enemies'. If this means that we are to have, or to try to work up, the kind of loving relationship we have with a member of our family, even more with a wife or husband, in which there are or ought to be pleasurable and physical expressions of our love, then I am quite sure we shall have to scrawl the word 'Impossible' upon it, whether it be the saying of Jesus or not. There is however a key to the dilemma here, it is this word 'love'. The New Testament is written in Greek, and Greek is a more subtle language than English. Jesus, of course, did not speak in Greek, but in Aramaic, a dialect of Hebrew, so knowing no Aramaic myself, I cannot say what word he may have used for love, but this I know, in this saying 'Love your enemies' there is used one of *the four words* in Greek that are translated by the one word 'love' in English and which has to do for them all, making of course for misunderstandings.

Now at the risk of sounding like a schoolmaster, let me tell you about these four words. First there is *storgē*. It is used to cover family affection such as that of a parent for a child or a child for a parent. It is natural love and occurs frequently

55

in classical Greek but not in the New Testament, and not here in Jesus' saying. Second, there is *eros*, describing the love of man for woman and vice versa. There is passion in it and it can turn into lust, which is often how it is understood today. This word does not occur in the New Testament anywhere. It means love with a burning, sometimes devastating longing. Third, there is *philia*. This occurs fairly frequently in the New Testament. It stands for real affection, even tender affection, including a kiss. As well as warmth it is compounded of esteem and respect. Matthew 10.37 (RSV) reads, 'He who loves father or mother more than me is not worthy of me', which the New English Bible renders, 'No man is worthy of me who cares more for father or mother than for me.' So *philio* means to care for. This again is not the word Jesus used according to the Greek in his saying 'Love your enemies'. He used the fourth word, *agapē*, which is a distinctive New Testament word for love and of frequent occurrence, and which does not appear outside the Bible and ecclesiastical books. Its real meaning is unconquerable benevolence, persistent goodwill.

We are now in a better position to understand the teaching of Jesus when he said, 'You have heard that it was said, "You shall love your neighbour and hate your enemy." But I say to you, Love your enemies and pray for those who persecute you.' He was not asking us to love our enemies as we love our nearest and dearest – it cannot be done. He was asking us to regard every person with persistent goodwill, indeed with benevolence, no matter how that person may have treated us; always we are to be concerned about his or her welfare. So when the jealous woman tries to take it out of us or the head of the rival firm across the road goes out of his way to make life awkward for us and to steal our profits, we shall not give way to hate, we shall exercise calm fair treatment always. This is how to love our enemies.

When the matter is put in this way it is obvious that this kind of love, the love Jesus in particular, and the New Testament in general, asks for is not something we can fall into, not something that comes to us 'out of the blue', hitting us, as it were. *Agapē* is not born of the emotions. No one *falls* in love with *agapē*, it is a product of the will. It is something we have to work at and may never wholly perfect, for it has to battle against the natural man in all of us. It is distinctive, the love which God has for us.

3 GOD'S LOVE FOR US

Now because it is God's love, we shall not love our enemies if we ourselves know nothing of God's love for us supremely revealed in Jesus Christ, for *agapē* is a reflection of it. This means that it is useless to *command* people to love their enemies, it cannot be done even if we understand what *agapē* is. When, however, we recognize that we are sinners, all of us, and free to receive God's forgiveness through the cross of Christ, even though we have been his enemies, we *acquire* the grace of God to accomplish the impossible, namely to love our enemies, and this includes that jealous man who persists in going out of his way to queer our pitch and that woman who can never resist making disparaging remarks about another woman's hairstyle.

Before leaving this striking saying of Jesus, let us note how he concludes what he had to say on his kind of love. We should pray for our enemies. This means we should not only allow them to do what they will to us, we should do something for them. We should pray for them, for who knows how miserable they may feel about what they are doing?

One last word, in case I should have so dealt with the battles in this sphere that are likely to come our way and therefore can appear to be trifling matters, let me tell you how one of our most famous commanders in the last war, who was normally of a remarkably equable temperament, really lost his temper one day. It came to his notice that some of his men had purposely left a bunch of prisoners without water though they suffered grievously and cried out for mercy. They were German prisoners, and the Germans had committed many atrocities in the war. But this high-ranking commander ordered them to be relieved at once and stood over his men to see that it was done forthwith. Was he a Christian commander? And did he know the words of Jesus, 'Love your enemies'? I shouldn't wonder. I should not wonder at all.

11
HOW NOT TO PRAY

In your prayers do not go babbling on like the heathen,
who imagine that the more they say the more likely they
are to be heard.
MATTHEW 6.7 (NEB)

When you first wake up in the morning, after you have
finished yawning (if you do), and before you have had that
first cup of tea (if you do), what should be your first thought
if you believe in God? Is it what jobs lie before you today,
that unfinished task in the kitchen? Or that pile of paperwork
on your desk, one of the banes of modern living? Or, of
course, it could be that that wretched pain from which you
suffer is still there, it hasn't cleared up overnight. Let me tell
you what your first thought should be. It is, 'God is present
with me today.'

Just that. When I was about nineteen I heard the then
Chaplain to the Forces say that every morning he jumped
out of bed, stood upright and said aloud, 'Glory be to the
Father and to the Son and to the Holy Ghost. Amen.' It
must have impressed me because I have never forgotten it.
No, I haven't managed that strenuous effort myself, but I do
say to myself each morning in bed before I do anything else
the opening words of the *Te Deum*, 'We praise thee O Lord,
We acknowledge thee to be the Lord.' I call this my daily act
of *reorientation*, for I believe reorientation to be the essence
of prayer, and prayer is what this sermon is going to be about
– first of all how not to do it. Hence my text, one of the
sayings of Jesus, 'In your prayers do not go babbling on like
the heathen, who imagine that the more they say the more
likely they are to be heard.' Or as the Authorized Version
words it, 'use not vain repetitions, as the heathen do'. The
original Greek has a strange word here, no one quite knows

59

what it means exactly. It is *battalogeō*, to 'stammer repeatedly'. Anyway, what is clear is that Jesus was telling his disciples, and us, how *not* to pray, 'Do not heap up empty phrases' (RSV), and we should certainly not be doing that in the early morning if we simply repeat the opening words of the *Te Deum* or say 'the Gloria', but it will be our daily reorientation.

1 WHEN PRAYER IS ABSURD

Now because my subject for this sermon, as I have already indicated, is prayer, you may be tempted to switch off. This is an activity for the very pious and therefore not for you. If so, you are wrong. You may not be very pious or even very religious, but let me tell you, most people at some time in their lives pray. Prayer is an almost universal human activity. Animals don't pray, but humans do. Why? Because life is fragile, liable at any time to be broken up, *and we know it*. Animals don't know it. Horses will go on grazing very soon after a calamity in which even some of them were involved, as if nothing had happened. Not so humans. Anxiety is never far below the surface of the human spirit. What will happen if I am made redundant? If I lose all my money? If our children run away from our home? A few days ago a woman came to ask my advice because she had received a letter from her granddaughter, aged twelve, complaining that her parents did not understand her and her father in particular scarcely ever spoke to her. Did this mean a family break-up was impending? And suppose my health deteriorates and I am left alone? Anxiety, yes, this is why people pray. If you read further on in St Matthew Chapter 6, from which my text is taken, you will find a whole paragraph about anxiety, anxiety about food, anxiety about clothes, anxiety about the future. Jesus knew how great is the part played by anxiety in people's lives because they feel so helpless. Then they turn to prayer, but then, alas, too often they make a great

60

mistake. They babble away, imagining that their many words will make God hear them. This is the heart of pagan religion, and Jesus spoke plainly about it to his followers. 'Do not imitate them,' he said.

In the Old Testament there is a telling story about babbling prayer. It centres on the prophet Elijah, who, according to the Epistle of James in the New Testament, was a man of prayer. You will find it in 1 Kings 18. The occasion was the contest between the prophet of the Lord, Elijah, and the prophets of the heathen god Baal championed by Ahab. It took place on Mount Carmel. Elijah made his challenge to the people, 'If the Lord is God, follow him; but if Baal, then follow him.' Since no response was forthcoming, Elijah ordered that a sacrificial altar be set up, replete with wood for burning and two bulls, but no fire. Then each of the parties were to invoke their god and the one who answered with fire would be God. The people agreed. So the prophets of Baal invoked their god. They did so from morning till noon, crying, 'Baal, Baal, answer us', but there was no sound, no answer. So they danced wildly beside the altar, Elijah all the while watching. And then he began to mock at this effusion of prayer: 'Call louder, for he is a god; it may be he is deep in thought, or engaged, or on a journey; or he may have gone to sleep and must be woken up.' If Elijah were mocking today he would probably say, 'Perhaps your god has gone to a cricket match or is watching television and mustn't be disturbed.' The prophets of Baal were goaded by the mockery to cry even louder and pile on more and yet more words, even to cut themselves with knives, but there was no sound, no answer, no sign of atten-tion. Of course there wasn't. There came a day when Jesus said it all: 'In your prayers do not go babbling on like the heathen, who imagine that the more they say the more likely they are to be heard.' It is an absurd idea, which is why Elijah on Mount Carmel mocked those who practised it. It was what the Latins call a *reductio ad absurdum* of prayer altogether.

2 HOW WE SHOULD PRAY

But how are we to pray? If we read on from Matthew Chapter 6 verse 7 we shall be told. 'Your Father knows what your needs are before you ask him.' And then this. 'This is how you should pray: "Our Father in heaven . . . "' How simple! How direct! How leagues away from badgering a remote and reluctant deity! But there is nothing cheap or familiar about this approach. The prayer goes on: 'Our Father in heaven, *thy name be hallowed.*' We call this the Lord's prayer. This is how Jesus prayed. He counted God as his Father. From the beginning of his ministry till the very end he lived in this consciousness. When at the age of twelve he was reproved by his mother for getting lost in the Temple, causing grave anxiety, he said, 'What made you search? Did you not know that I was bound to be in my Father's house?' (Luke 2.49). And when he was dying on the cross he prayed, 'Father, into thy hands I commit my spirit' (Luke 23.46). Prayer for Jesus was first of all living and even dying in the divine Father's presence, and that same God is our Father too. 'This is how you should pray,' said Jesus to his disciples, and the word he used for father was the Aramaic word 'Abba', for Aramaic was the language which Jesus habitually spoke.

Now what does it mean to count God as 'Our Father'? First, that God is not remote, up above the clouds. A father is accessible, he is part of the family. One does not have to arrange an appointment to make contact with him, access is immediate. What is more, it is natural to be able to speak to him about the most ordinary everyday matters, even trivial concerns. One doesn't make prepared speeches to one's father. That God, then, the creator and sustainer of the universe is 'Our Father' is a quite astounding assertion, but Jesus made it and lived by it. 'Our Father in heaven, hallowed be thy name,' perhaps the most widely and generally known of all Jesus' sayings. We need to let the implication of this sink in.

Jesus was of course speaking out of his own experience of Joseph as his father. In Jewish families the father was the most significant and important leader. He was the undisputed head. He bore the responsibility for the maintenance of the home, took an active part in the children's upbringing, including of course religion, helped the adolescents to a trade or profession, and conducted the regular Friday night prayers. Today in the modern world we hear much about absent fathers; there is even a view that apart from the act of procreation fathers are scarcely necessary, they are dispensable, and some much prefer to have it so. All this was and is unthinkable in Jewish homes. The father was a responsible, caring and highly respected figure. Jesus lived with this concept of fatherhood in the home at Nazareth, and when he came to call God 'Our Father' it was replete with overtones drawn from experience.

I think perhaps one of the most telling pictures of the Fatherhood of God is in the parable of the prodigal son which Jesus told. In reading or hearing this we concentrate on the wayward son, hence the title given to the parable, and possibly, though to a lesser extent, we give our attention to the elder self-righteous brother. But what about the father? He is a picture of God as Jesus understood him. He was not repressive, he gave the younger son his freedom, he did not block his escape into the 'far country' to waste his substance with riotous living, he let him go. But he was forever looking up that road by which the son had gone, hoping to see the boy returning. And the day came when he did; he spied him in rags, shuffling along the homeward path, and ran to meet him – yes, ran, how undignified! – flung his arms round him, and kissed him. This is the picture Jesus gave of God, and this is the proper picture for us to have of God, our caring, loving, freedom-giving Father. This is what Jesus would have us understand. This is what we should have in mind when we take up his saying, 'Our Father in heaven, hallowed be thy name.' This is how we should pray.

63

3 EXTENDED PRAYER

But is this all? Is that short, almost ejaculatory prayer in the early morning sufficient? It is not. We read in the gospels of a number of times Jesus prayed. There was that evening at the very beginning of his ministry in Galilee when the crowds swarmed around him in excited expectancy, bringing their sick. And he healed them, but as soon as it was daylight he escaped to a lonely spot in order to engage in prayer. Then again after his cure of a leper, an unheard of thing, we read that from time to time he would withdraw to lonely places for prayer. So Jesus prayed both at times of pressing need and when he was eminently successful. After the feeding of the five thousand with bread in a desert place he left the astonished crowds and went up the hillside to pray. What was this? Was it to keep in touch with his heavenly Father and not be caught in a trap of self-esteem at a time of popularity? Perhaps not surprisingly we are told that he spent the night in prayer prior to choosing his twelve disciples, for it was a turning point in his whole mission. Not surprisingly too was it, when it became clear that his life was nearing its end, that he took three of his disciples and went up the hillside to pray; that came to be called the Mount of Transfiguration.

In addition to these special occasions Jesus kept the statutory times of corporate prayer, and doubtless like every Jew he repeated the *Shema* at every daybreak, 'Hear, O Israel, the Lord our God is one Lord . . . ' Yes, Jesus' praying was simple, but its simplicity was not its brevity, but the fact of its unvarying directness of approach to his heavenly Father. This was his secret. This should be our secret in prayer.

And now this – if we are caring Christians, our prayers cannot be brief though never wordy. There are so many people in our hearts and minds whose needs we wish to bring before our heavenly Father. People we know intimately and people of whom we only hear and read about in the newspapers. The hungry and the millions whose lives are ruined by war, and some persecuted on account of their colour or religion. We shall not 'babble away' to God on their behalf. God knows their trouble, but his power is only able to be received if there are hands stretched forth in expectation. This is where intercessory prayer operates; and not only individual prayer, but corporate prayer, prayer by the Church, prayer by a praying group. Not that it compounds the pressure on God, but a community praying together strengthens the praying by the support which togetherness brings.

*   *   *

It is time I finished this sermon, it has already been overlong, so let me end with an extended saying of Jesus, indeed a parable about unreal prayer. Two men went up to the Temple to pray, one a religious type, the other a member of the corrupt and therefore hated tax-gathering profession of his time. The religious one stood up and prayed thus:

> 'I thank thee, O God, that I am not like the rest of men, greedy, dishonest, adulterous . . . I fast twice a week; I pay tithes on all that I get.' But the other kept his distance and would not even raise his eyes to heaven, but beat upon his breast, saying, 'O God, have mercy on me, sinner that I am.'
> (Luke 18.11–13, NEB)

It was only the second man who really prayed. There were few words, but God was the focus of his attention, not himself. No matter how many words are employed and how much unction spilled over, no prayer is being offered unless the consciousness of God's real presence is there. This is the heart of the matter. We must not forget it.

12

BE CAREFUL ABOUT SEEING

The lamp of the body is the eye.
MATTHEW 6.22–23 (NEB)

Some weeks ago there came into my hands some chapters of a book about Audrey Hepburn. You will not be surprised if I tell you that my normal reading is not about film stars, but this happened to come my way and my attention was caught by her picture on the cover, especially her eyes, wide apart, alive and searching. Apparently an American film producer, seeing those eyes in a picture, said, 'I must have her for my next film, I have searched all over Europe and America for a face with eyes like that.' But Audrey Hepburn was more than a pretty face. True, she knew comfort, her mother came from a long line of Dutch nobility, but she also knew suffering. During the German occupation of Belgium she and her family, like thousands of other people, were reduced to near starvation, subsisting for long periods on tulip bulbs for food. But Audrey Hepburn did not succumb. She joined the Belgian Resistance and spent herself on the side in relieving distress wherever she found it. And this is the point I am coming to, you could see this depth of character and compassion in her eyes. They weren't simply beautiful. They were a window on what she really was, an index of her soul. Or, in the saying of Jesus, 'the lamp of the body is the eye.'

1 THE INDEX OF CHARACTER

What this means is that the eye is the first part of a man or woman to notice when seeking to judge character and resource. Some people's eyes are dim, they do not appear to be 'taking in' (as we say) what they are seeing. Ask them what they saw on holiday, the towns they visited, the countryside they passed through, and they will be able to tell you very little. It is not that they wear spectacles, a visit to the oculist would do nothing for them. The truth is they are sluggish people. Their eyes tell you this as soon as you meet them. 'The lamp of the body is the eye.' And some people's eyes are shifty. We should be wary about entrusting ourselves, our word, or our property, to them. They will turn out to be unreliable, but worse than that, deceitful. Notice people's eyes when you encounter them. They will tell you much. And then there are people with angry eyes. With only the slightest provocation they glare at you. Cross their paths even in the slightest of ways and they will flare up at once. These people love confrontation, they are bored by tranquillity, they revel in battle. Do not expect balanced judgement or behaviour from such people. And utterly different from them are people, men and women, with a twinkle in their eyes; there is laughter hidden there and a predisposition to merriment. These people make good company, even if it is not possible to count on their wisdom or intelligence, but they have something of value to give to the community. And there are compassionate eyes, eyes that speak of love, and intelligent eyes notable for their concentration, evidenced perhaps by a slight frown. We have by no means exhausted the variety of human eyes that there are, male and female, but surely enough has been said to establish the force of Jesus' saying, 'The lamp of the body is the eye.' We can be certain he always took good care to notice the eyes of the people he encountered. It is true there is very little in the gospel narrations to tell us about him physically, but we do read how intently he looked at people. He used his eyes. They were a lamp on people.

2 SEEING SHAPES CHARACTER

My first point then, deriving from the saying of Jesus, 'The lamp of the body is the eye,' is that it is the index of character and we should be wise to take note of people's eyes, for they tell us much.

My second point is that the way we use our eyes will determine to no small extent the kind of people we have become. If you are a wise parent, you will take good care what you let your children see. It isn't easy, especially if they have their own television set. I bring in the fact of television at once because it is one of the dominant features of the age in which we live. Masses of people are 'glued' to television. They watch it for hours every day. In some homes it is never switched off. If, then, what we see determines to no small extent what we become – 'The lamp of the body is the eye' – those people are not far wrong who maintain that it is difficult to judge how far television has been a blessing to society and how far a curse. There are indeed some splendid programmes on television, beautiful, entertaining and informative, but there are others which are disgraceful, they portray pornography, violence and crime and cannot fail to have an effect on the watching community at large. The truth is modern technology has enabled us to see the good, bad and indifferent as never before in the world's history. So the saying of Jesus, 'The lamp of the body is the eye,' is extremely relevant to our time. It forces upon us the question, 'What do we allow ourselves to see?'

Behind this is another question, and interlocking with it. What do we want to see? Regretfully there are some people who have eyes for nothing but sex. Now sex is a good thing, it is a proper part of life, and it cannot be blotted out, but

68

when it is allowed to dominate almost every activity, as if it were the 'be all and end all' of existence, it corrupts. There is an old Latin tag which reads, *Corruptio optimi pessima*, the corruption of the best is the worst. This is true of sex. All the more reason then *how* we let it dominate our seeing.

What I have been saying is perhaps a *glaring* instance of the relevance today of the saying, 'The lamp of the body is the eye.' Let me turn to more ordinary illustrations. It is easy to fall into the trap of always seeing the worst in situations and the worst in people. Two years ago I got caught out on this myself – please forgive a homely illustration. I had taken particular trouble with the garden that year because I knew my wife was failing in health (she has died since) and I wanted it to give her much pleasure, and it did. More than once she commented on the smoothness of the lawns and the profusion of colour in the flower beds. But I knew of the failures there were and the parts of the garden it was best not to see. And wishing perhaps not to sound too pleased with my efforts I often referred to them. Then she rebuked me, very gently. She was gentle over everything she did. But it was a rebuke. 'Why do you always see the failures and not the beauty that is everywhere?' She was right. 'The lamp of the body is the eye.' What is it that we see in the world around us and in people? The ugly, the distorted, the neglected, the failures? We should use our eyes to see the good, then we shall feel good and goodness will be the atmosphere around us and we shall even contribute to it. What we choose to see is a governing factor in life more influential than we probably realize. 'The lamp of the body is the eye.'

3 DOUBLE DARKNESS

Now let me complete this penetrating saying of Jesus in the way it is given in St Matthew's gospel. 'The lamp of the body is the eye. If your eyes are sound, you will have light for your whole body; if the eyes are bad, your whole body will be in darkness. If then the only light you have is darkness, the darkness is doubly dark.'

There can be little doubt but that Jesus was goaded to say this by the behaviour of the general run of the religious teachers of his day, chiefly the lawyers and the Pharisees. He denounced them soundly according to Matthew Chapter 23, calling them hypocrites and blind guides, yet they set themselves up as leaders of the people. These men were spiritually blind, their eyes were bad; and what was worse, they were responsible for their blindness. They were determined not to recognize Jesus as a man sent from God, they even went so far as to maintain that he was inspired by the devil (Mark 3.22). Was it that they saw Jesus as a rival to their position in the community? In the end they came to plot his removal from their midst. So the light that was in them became darkness and it was doubly dark.

Jesus epitomized this whole situation with a striking saying, 'Can the blind lead the blind; shall they not both fall into the ditch?' One New Testament commentator (I forget who) has made this memorable with a word picture. Two blind men were shuffling happily along a footpath, holding each other's arms. They reckoned they would be all right had they not mutual support? Boldly they strode along. They knew the way, or thought they did. The path was flanked by a ditch, but 'not to worry', they knew about this and would keep out of its way. True, they hesitated from time to time, and people watching wondered if they would come to a halt, but no, they went on. They hesitated, but still they went on, confident of their progress. What they did not know, however, was that at one point the ditch took a sharp turn, and they of course went straight on. And then those watching did not know whether to laugh or cry. Down went one into the ditch, and then the other grasping him went down too. Their mutual support was useless, just as Jesus said, 'Can the blind lead the blind; shall they not both fall into the ditch?'

There is a warning here. It is to beware of people who reckon they know the way to a satisfying life – money, pleasure, sexual liberty, popularity, complete freedom to go one's own way regardless. If they have no regard for Christ in the way they recommend, they will not know the light of life, and eventually darkness will close around them. Deliberately *to refuse* to see Christ means double darkness, however learned or attractive the teacher may be.

I began this sermon by emphasizing the importance of our eyes. 'The lamp of the body is the eye.' What we see determines to some extent the kind of people we are and become. And we have control over what we see and allow ourselves to see. I mentioned television. I want to finish by saying, 'Make sure you can see Christ.' I mean choose to see him, take trouble to see him. You will not understand him altogether. He is beyond that, but we should see him as the light of the world, the light of life. I cannot resist the temptation to end with a chorus sometimes sung at children's services. Childish it may be, but there is profundity in it:

Turn your eyes upon Jesus
Look full in his wonderful face
And the things of earth will grow strangely dim
In the light of his glory and grace.

'The lamp of the body is the eye.' Take care what you see.

13

THE MASTERY OF WORRY

Sufficient unto the day is the evil thereof.
MATTHEW 6.34 (AV)

This is one of the most cryptic of Jesus' sayings, so cryptic we go scurrying to the modern versions to see if they will help. There is the Revised Standard Version's rendering, 'Let the day's own trouble be sufficient for the day.' There is the New English Bible's wording, 'Each day has troubles enough of its own.' Both help, and we shall be wise to use them, but it has to be admitted that the Authorized Version's 'Sufficient unto the day is the evil thereof' is as close as can be to six Greek words reporting what Jesus actually said, though of course he spoke in Aramaic, not in Greek. Apparently Jesus did employ hard sayings in his conversation, hard not least in their form of expression. But because they puzzled they were remembered.

1 THE PUNCH LINE

Actually this cryptic saying is the punch line at the end of an extended teaching phrase. Obviously it was not only meant to be remembered, but also to draw together all that he had been saying. Punch lines are meant to do that. The subject was not abstruse, it was anxiety, one of the commoner of human maladies, especially in the modern world. The section begins, 'Therefore I tell you, do not be anxious about your life, what you shall eat or what you shall drink, nor about your body, what you shall put on.' These will probably not be the matters we shall worry about in our modern world, though this question, 'What shall I wear?' will never be far away from the feminine members of the community. Our worries are more likely to concern mortgage rates of interest, redundancy and the consequent loss of income, or it could be that man or that woman in the office we cannot be sure we can trust, or that girl our son is going about with and who is not suitable for him, or that pain in the back which makes the problem of shopping loom large in the future, or what to do about aged parents, or the children's schooling, and marriage ties obviously progressively wearing more and more thin. Problems like this keep people awake at night. At four o'clock in the morning they go over points again and again, and of course are so weary the next day that even the ordinary and easy affairs become a burden. Worry has physical consequences. It is not by accident that the two typical diseases of modern life are stomach ulcers and thrombosis. So when Jesus spoke at some length about anxiety, capping it with the punch line, 'Sufficient unto the day is the evil thereof,' he was not handling some rare human problem, but one of the commonest and most damaging. The number of people who know nothing about worry must be very few indeed.

2 WORRY IS NATURAL FOR HUMAN BEINGS

Worry, however, is natural, that is to say it is natural for human beings. It is an index, indeed a consequence, of sensitivity and intelligence. Animals don't worry, which is not to say that they lack feeling. I shall not forget two horses in the field next to our garden. They had the place all to themselves all day, and although they were very different breeds and different in age they were the greatest of friends and were constantly playing with each other with biting, pushing and shoving as part of their fun. Then the younger and more virile of the two was considered too expensive to keep and was sold. I remember how for three whole days the one left behind cried. We grew weary of his cries. Clearly he felt the loss enormously, but the pain was immediate, there were no preliminaries and no consequences. An animal lives in the present, which is why it knows nothing about worry. We humans, on the contrary, are very aware of our past which has become part of us and very aware of our future which is unknown. This is our problem, the ground of our anxiety. How shall we manage, if, when and supposing . . . We go over it again and again in bed.

And now we turn to this sixth chapter of St Matthew and to Jesus' words, 'Therefore I bid you put away anxious thoughts about food and drink to keep you alive, and clothes to cover your body . . . Look at the birds of the air; they do not sow and reap and store in barns, yet your heavenly Father feeds them.' Yes, but we aren't birds of the air, we aren't horses, we are human beings, we have to sow, reap and store in barns, if we didn't we should be in a poor way. It is all very well for Jesus calmly to say, 'Put away anxious thoughts.' We can't, we are human beings, worry is natural to us, but we are aware of the need to control our worries, for they can be devastating. The question is how, how can we control our worries?

3 NECESSITIES FOR CONTROLLING WORRY

First, we need a lively sense of God, the great creator and sustainer of the universe, as *our heavenly Father*. This isn't easy, but it is basic. It means realizing that we are not alone in the world, not alone in the events which actually surround us. There is a divine Presence closer even than our worries and sympathizing with them even if they are unworthy. Here is a schoolboy worried about that examination he has to sit in a few weeks' time. He keeps his anxiety to himself, he is not sure his parents would understand, but then one day he lets out his worry. He talks, the parents comment, not for very long, but very simply and kindly with no chiding thrown in. And the worry shared became a worry lifted, if not completely removed, but on the way to being mastered, which is a subject in itself. None of this is possible without the first step, believing, holding on to the belief that we have a heavenly Father who understands and cares.

Second, we need to see the futility of worry. It accomplishes nothing at all. Jesus uttered another of his arresting sayings to drive home this point. 'Is there a man of you who by anxious thought can add a foot to his height? Or, as the Authorized Version has it, 'Which of you by being anxious can add one cubit to his stature?' For myself I much prefer this rendering, it seems more intelligent. I mean, who would want to add a foot, twelve inches, to his height! Very, very few men, and no woman. The operative word here is *helikia* in the Greek, which can mean 'length of life'. So the saying makes sense: 'Which of you by being anxious and worrying about it can prolong your life?' Surely the truth is that by worrying we are far more likely to shorten our days on this earth, not lengthen them. So worry is futile. It accomplishes nothing. The crying need then is to learn how to master it.

4 A DAY AT A TIME

So we come to the punch line, 'Sufficient unto the day . . . ' We must learn to live a day at a time. This does not mean we must forgo all planning in our lives. We cannot. Some of us have had to live for years with diaries packed with engagements even a year ahead and more. And if there were no financial planning our lives would break down in disaster. But we must not fall into the trap of trying to live in and through those days ahead, not even tomorrow. 'Sufficient unto the day', said Jesus. This is how he lived. This is why he was serene. He believed that the grace and power would come when needed. He relied on 'his Father'. And this is what we must do. Plan tomorrow, yes, we must; but do not try to live tomorrow, leave it till it comes.

Since Jesus was talking about anxiety it is not surprising that *troubles* should dominate his saying, 'Each day has troubles enough of its own.' But all our days are not replete with troubles. The skies are not perpetually cloudy. There are glorious days full of sunshine. And there are days when we meet friends and have some good laughs. This is his message. Enjoy those good days to the full. Not all the days will be joyous like that. Perhaps tomorrow won't be. So live a day at a time, not allowing the unknown of tomorrow to cloud over today. And let me add this. Be thankful for small kindnesses that unexpectedly come our way. Yesterday when I was coming out of church and getting into my car, a lady whom I knew by sight, but not more, came up to me holding a paper bag with a present inside. No, not a learned work on Greek philosophy, but two jars of marmalade she had made. That small homely act made my day. I let it warm my heart. Sufficient unto the day . . .

And remember this. You can't really be an efficient man or woman whatever your calling in life, whether it be managing a big business with endless demands on your time or a mother in the home. Worry spoils the quality and the amount of work which can be accomplished. And if you have to employ someone or choose a man or woman with whom to work, you won't of course 'go for' the happy-go-lucky type. With him or her there are bound to be troubles. But don't go for the worrier either. That perpetual frown will tell you something. Success for such a person will be limited. Worry militates against success.

So then, 'Sufficient unto the day . . . ', this is the key to the control of worry. And if we do control it, I can tell you something. We shall be strong characters. Make no mistake about it. Jesus was very strong. He did not worry (according to John 14.27), not even on the night before his crucifixion, which he knew was at hand. 'Peace I leave with you,' he said to his disciples, 'my peace I give unto you. Let not your heart be troubled, neither let it be afraid.'

I come back to the punch line. I must if I am to follow the pattern of preaching Jesus perfected, the punch line which sums up what he had to say about worry. 'Sufficient unto the day is the evil thereof.'

14

THE EXERCISE OF DISCRIMINATION

*Give not that which is holy unto the dogs, neither cast ye
your pearls before swine, lest they trample them under their
feet, and turn again rend you.*

MATTHEW 7.6 (AV)

I have looked long and hard at this saying of Jesus embedded
in what is called the Sermon on the Mount, and I cannot for
the life of me see what connection it has with what precedes
or follows it. Nothing therefore, for me at any rate, is to be
gleaned from the context to help with its interpretation or
even when or why Jesus uttered it. Not that this detracts from
its authenticity, on the contrary its stark isolation reinforces
it. My guess is that out of the host of Jesus' sayings, most of
them unrecorded, which those hundreds and hundreds of
people who heard him in person remembered after he was no
longer with them, a collection was made, probably more than
one, and when St Matthew's gospel came to be written the
author incorporated sayings from such a collection, and in it
was this saying about not casting your pearls before the
swine. He had to include it because it was so striking and so
obviously authentic. But where was it to be placed in the
gospel record? There was nothing to indicate when or where
or even why Jesus uttered it. So it was placed in the Sermon
on the Mount, so called, sitting there now in the text all on its
own, even awkwardly and tantalizingly. Or does verse 11, a
little further on in the text, chime in with it? 'If you, then, bad
as you are, know how to give your children what is good for
them . . . ' (NEB). 'Bad as you are' – was Jesus boldly realistic
like this in his estimate of human nature? Apparently he
labelled *some* of them swine! So there was nothing sloppy,
sentimental or even cosy about him. He was a realist. This is
what this strange saying says to us first of all, and if we wish

to know what he, the historical Jesus, was like, we had better take this blunt saying on board.

1 THE FORM OF THE SAYING

But did he really speak like this? Listen to the words again:

Give not that which is holy unto the dogs,
neither cast ye your pearls before swine,
lest they trample them under their feet,
and turn again and rend you.

It has poetic form, and if you think about it you will see that the first line is complemented by the fourth and the second by the third (by the way, the NEB fails to show this). Apparently Jesus sometimes spoke in this rhythmic way in order to make what he said memorable. After all, there was no one to take it down in shorthand. If, however, he said what he had to say many times, its rhythm made it stick in people's minds, which is precisely what he wanted.

Some scholars tell us that the symmetry in this saying is spoiled by the word 'holy' in line one. The original could as readily be translated 'earring', 'Do not give an earring unto the dogs' (as you put a ring in a pig's snout). I don't know, but I see the argument. Anyway, the meaning is clear: exercise discrimination in what you give people.

2 PREACHERS MUST READ PEOPLE FIRST

First and foremost this saying of Jesus bears on the preaching of the gospel. There has to be discrimination to whom it is presented, otherwise more harm than good will come of it. A clear warning for the over-enthusiastic evangelist. Enthusiasm is good, indeed there can be little effective evangelism without it, but not everyone is suitable to be the recipient of the message such an evangelical has to give. Some people, perhaps many people, lack the capacity to grasp anything at a spiritual level. They are earthy and have ears only for what is material and sexual. To approach such people with the gospel, however much they may stand in need of it, is not only a waste of time and effort, it is to invite ridicule and mockery. This means that the preacher must be able to read people and sense situations, whether he is making contact with an individual or a crowd.

Is this why Jesus addressed the multitudes (as they are called in the gospels) in parables? It was in order that those in the crowd who were spiritually deaf heard nothing they could grasp, even though it intrigued them, and therefore nothing they could mock. Doubtless they simply shrugged their shoulders and went on thinking about their sheep or their fishing expedition. So if you are looking for a preacher for your church or an evangelist in the community, make sure first of all that he/she can read people and know when to speak and when to hold their tongue.

I expect you have noticed, if you are a reader of the gospels, that Jesus had nothing to say to King Herod when a prisoner in his hands, and very little to say to Pontius Pilate. Herod Antipas was a playboy and Pilate had very little room for anything else in his thinking but the security or insecurity of his position as the Roman governor of the turbulent province of Judaea. Unthinking readers might suggest how wonderful it would have been for the progress of the gospel if Jesus had given his testimony to these two, better still if they were converted in consequence. But Jesus held his tongue. He said nothing. He knew better. His words would have no effect. Neither Herod nor Pilate would be changed. They never would be. There are people to whom it would be useless even for the Son of God to preach. It is a sobering thought, 'writing people off' in this way, but we have to accept it. Jesus took good care not to give that which is holy to the dogs nor to cast his pearls before the swine so that they could trample them under their feet; but they did turn and rend him all the same.

3 TALKING AND DOING

And now something else. We may gather from this saying that Jesus was sparing with words. He was not a great talker. He never spoke loosely. Great talkers are not sensitive people. They do not note the reaction of their hearers to what they are saying. They 'plough' on regardless. This is because their prime concern is with themselves, not with the men and women who have to listen to them. Not so Jesus. He read people, read their eyes, read them at a glance – the sufferer with a disease longing for healing, the widow frightened of the future because of the loss of her son, the women bringing their children to him to be blessed. He did not preach to them, he simply took the children in his arms. If Jesus was not a great talker in the sense of being a loose and compulsive talker, he was a great doer. He did what he saw each person needed, the leper, the woman with a haemorrhage embarrassing her and wearing her down, the deaf mute who could not even say what he wanted.

There is a lesson here for us. We have been shocked that Jesus wrote off some people, perhaps many people, as hopeless as far as receiving the good news of the gospel was concerned. Are we then to wash our hands of these people? Are they to be left without any rescue line in the rough seas of life, no hope for the future, no eternal destiny beyond the grave? No, they are not to be abandoned. If they cannot respond to words they will respond to deeds, which often speak louder than words. This is why Jesus in his ministry in Galilee and Judaea worked what are commonly, and not very accurately, called his miracles. They were really signs that God cared for the broken and deformed, and signs is what such actions are called in the Greek accounts in the gospels, signs of God's presence and God's love. The preacher, the evangelist, must be ready with actions on behalf of people, words alone will not do.

I have been reading recently about a young housewife who

81

through the sitting-room window of her house on the sea front noticed a woman about her own age who came day after day and stood motionless on the beach, staring out to sea. The sight not only perplexed her, it worried her. She could have drawn the curtains and shut her out of her mind, after all it was no business of hers, but somehow she couldn't. So next time she saw her there she took her courage in her hands and went down to the woman. It was a creature of obvious sadness that she found, needing very gentle handling if anything was to be achieved at all. But gently, very gently, she showed her concern to see her standing there day after day just looking out to sea, a picture of hopelessness. With consummate tact she managed to coax her up the cliff to her home, where she encouraged her to talk. 'You must tell someone,' she said, 'if you are to surmount your trouble.' At that her story came out. She had lost her husband at sea, one day he never came back, and when after a while she tried to rebuild her broken life and live for her son, a small boy aged two, he died suddenly of meningitis. She felt she had nothing left at all, her life was nothing but a meaningless blank. But although she did not know it then, there was something left. To cut a long story short, in time she became a competent schoolteacher again, especially good with difficult children. It all began with the woman who had spied her on the beach and who did not shrug her shoulders and say it was no business of hers.

4 GOOD AND BAD IN HUMAN NATURE

And now another point to notice about Jesus arising out of his strange but arresting saying, 'Give not that which is holy unto the dogs, neither cast ye your pearls before swine.' Yes, Jesus saw human nature realistically with all its fickleness, faithlessness, and glaring failures, but he did not take a gloomy view, and certainly no a jaundiced view. Yes, he did not hold back from calling people swine and some of them dogs, and he was not thinking of the cuddly household pet dogs, but the dangerous street scavenger mongrels that roamed the streets of Eastern towns and villages. But if you read on from verse 6 in St Matthew Chapter 7 you will discover at verse 11 that he also said this, 'If you, bad as you are, know how to give good gifts to your children . . . ' So in Jesus' view not even the bad were bad through and through, they have goodness somewhere in them and Jesus recognized it. He could read people. I think the truth of this mixture in human nature sometimes comes out in the rough and crude public concerns for animals. I read not long ago of a brute of a man, a very devil to work for, but he had a dog, and when one day the dog died he wept like a child, to the astonishment and bewilderment of his subordinates. Jesus recognized this strange mixture in human nature, bad and good mixed up together. Was there perhaps even in those tough and cruel Nazi tormentors a soft spot somewhere? I wonder. What I want to say is this, God does not overlook the tiniest whisp of goodness, wherever it is found.

★ ★ ★

But be careful. Yes, there is good and bad in all of us. But don't imagine we can tot up our good points and balance them against our bad points on the strength of which we can qualify, even by a narrow margin, for the reward of eternal life. No one can earn this. We can only have it as a gift received through faith in Christ, who died for us all that we might possess it.

15

GOOD FOUNDATIONS

Every one then who hears these words of mine and does them will be like a wise man who built his house upon the rock.
MATTHEW 7.24 (RSV)

I have never built a house, and I don't suppose you have, unless you happen to be a builder by trade, and women as a rule don't build houses, though in these days of DIY we all look after them ourselves, men and women. We don't how-ever need any professional knowledge or skill to understand these words of Jesus, but what we do need, however, is a little information about house building in Jesus' day in Palestine. In a number of places the temptation was to site one's house down by a stream, and understandably. The sandy ground was soft there, obviating the time-consuming and laborious task of digging out the foundations. The house could be constructed in a short time, and with the water and the stream nearby the carrying of the water for the stone- or brick-laying would be a fairly simple matter. But suppose a site further back were chosen, at a higher level, well above the winter flood level and where rocks abounded. The builder who worked there could be mocked by the builder at the lower level. He would have finished his house, maybe even be living in it, enjoying the pleasant prospect out across the water, while the builder up on the rock would still be sweating away on walls hardly above foundation level, if that. Well and good, but wait till the spring and autumn rains come, and the tearing wind. Who has the last laugh then? Wind and incessant rain are disastrous for any building whose foundation is on sandy soil. It simply collapses, and when that happens the man who built it will think what a fool he was not to have sited his house higher up with foundations built into the rocky ground. True, it was far easier to build on the sand, but wisdom counsels that the more difficult task of building with a rock foundation is by far the best plan in the long run.

1 HARD FOUNDATION SAYINGS

According to the way St Matthew has arranged his material in his gospel the word picture about house building is placed at 7.24, at the end of the collection of Jesus' sayings commonly called the Sermon on the Mount. There are some hard sayings in it, for example, 'Blessed are the meek, for they shall inherit the earth,' and, 'You have heard that it was said, "You shall not commit adultery." But I say to you that every one who looks at a woman lustfully has already committed adultery with her in his heart,' and, 'You have heard that it was said, "An eye for an eye and a tooth for a tooth." But I say to you, Do not resist one who is evil. But if any man strikes you on the right cheek, turn to him the other also.' We can mock at the man trying to live by these almost monstrous injunctions, and others like them, or even taking them seriously. Far easier to swim with the tide in the matters of morals. Let prevailing custom determine where or how we shall build our houses. And that is true. But what about when life turns nasty – and it does sometimes – and the tearing winds howl, rattling our structures, and the torrential rains sweep away our feeble resistance? Then, according to Jesus' saying, the man or woman who builds on the hard precepts is the wise person and the foolish one is he or she who consistently takes the easy path in the matter of behaviour or morals.

This then is what Jesus said about his own sayings. Some are very hard, but we shall be wise to build our lives on them. Hear the text again: 'Every one then who hears these words of mine and does them will be like a wise man who built his house upon the rock.'

2 NOT RULES OF BEHAVIOUR

And now let me draw your attention to something else in this and the following verse. There is no suggestion that any directions were given as to where the two respective and contrasting builders were to site their houses. They were at perfect liberty to follow their own inclinations and preferences. There was no one to stop them, not even a borough council or an environmental specialist. Everything turns on the word 'wisdom'. Where and how is it wise to build?

It is a great mistake to read the sayings in the Sermon on the Mount as if they were laws or rules of behaviour. They are not. Let me take one saying from the collection to demonstrate this. 'You have heard that it was said, "You shall not commit adultery".' There is a rule for you down in black and white! So you might think. Now listen to Jesus. His way is different. 'But' – notice the 'but' – 'But I say to you that every one who looks at a woman lustfully has already committed adultery with her in his heart.' It is a descriptive statement, not more not less. What happens when a man sees all women as prospective sexual partners? He may protest, 'Ah, but I don't actually use women like this.' Maybe not, in normal times, but what about when the storms blow up? An unexpected opportunity presents itself. He loses his head because it is full of eroticism, he is swept off his feet, and the result is the collapse of his marriage and even the loss of his job. We are not without cases of this kind with some public men whose names are familiar. And the cry goes up, 'How could he be so foolish?' Ah, but he has built his house on the sand, that is on his moods and sexual urges. Why shouldn't he? There is no one to stop him, and he can feed his mind on pornographic literature and films, there are opportunities today in plenty. Then one day the storms of passion overwhelm him. He would have been wise to build his house, his life, on the rock of the sayings of Jesus and not on shifting sands or mere emotion. No, there are no laws in

Jesus' teachings. Each one of us is free to do as we like. The basic question, however, is, 'What form of conduct is wise?' Let each judge for himself or herself. There are the sayings of Jesus to help us make up our minds.

'Every one then who hears these words of mine and does them' – yes, and does them – 'will be like a wise man who built his house upon the rock.'

3 FIRM BUT FLEXIBLE

Now this metaphor of a building with a sure foundation built on the rock is not the only one Jesus employed. He made use of all kinds of metaphors. There was the sower sowing his seed, there was the sheep wandering away from the fold and becoming lost, there was the merchant seeking fine pearls and when he finds an outstanding one he sells all and buys that one. All of them metaphors taken from common life. And so we should not take the metaphor of the house built on the rock as the one and only to picture our lives. Where it lacks is in its rigidity, proper to a house but not to everything.

We who live in Surrey well remember the great wind storm of October 1987, a great surprise to us. We don't have hurricanes in this part of the country, but we had one that night and we shall never forget it. It made havoc of our orchards and gardens. My garden was a shambles. With trepidation, at first light I went to look at our huge weeping willow tree quite close to the house. I hardly dared look. Had it crashed into the house and ruined the structure? It had not, it was completely unbroken except for a few small branches. And of course the reason was a willow tree bends and sways with the wind. It is not rigid, there is give in it. Provided it is well rooted it is surprising what storms it will stand. And this is the lesson for us. We need to be well rooted in the sayings of Jesus, but we need also to be flexible. We must not be rigid.

At the present time in church circles there is a great debate in progress about fundamentalism and liberalism. The one is very fixed in its theological thinking and practice, the other has its theology and practice shaped to some extent by the fashions of the times in which we live. What I wish to commend is neither of these alternatives, but what I will call a positive approach. Some of the tenets of our faith are basic, they are fundamental, they are like the foundation of a house. It cannot, it must not, be tampered with or the whole structure will be endangered. I refer to such beliefs as God as the creator, Jesus as the incarnate Son of God, the salvation of mankind by Christ's cross and passion, the truth of his resurrection, and presence of his Spirit in the world always, and the life of the world to come. We cannot give way on these, but in matters of conduct we must exhibit a certain flexibility, we must be willing to bend, above all we must be ready to accept as brothers and sisters those who to some degree think and act differently from us. Too much rigidity drives people away; too liberal an approach fails to gather them in. In between there is what I have called a positive approach. It is well rooted in the Christian faith, but because like the weeping willow tree in my garden it is able to bend it does not break in the storm and come crashing down.

There came to see me the other day a retired deputy head-mistress of a large infant school, as we used to call them. She was married and had children of her own, now grown up. When they were young they were often naughty and in adolescence and young manhood and womanhood some of their activities did not meet with her approval. She was worried by this and it was clear from her conversation with me that the whole question of when to bend and when not to bend in relation to their activities worried her. I think she took the right course. She told them she did not like the way they were living but ended, 'I shall go on loving you whatever you do.' Jesus surely stretched this overriding principle to the utmost limit when he said – and you will find this saying in the same Sermon on the Mount we have been considering – 'Love your enemies and pray for those who persecute you, so that you may be sons of your Father who is in heaven; for he makes his sun rise on the evil and on the good, and sends rain on the just and on the unjust' (Matthew 5.44–45, RSV).

Yes, we must build our lives on a firm foundation, but we must not be completely unbending, and we shall not be if we are motivated by love. This is positive Christian behaviour.

16

THE EXTENT OF GOD'S CARE

Are not sparrows two a penny? Yet without your
Father's leave not one of them can fall to the ground.
As for you, even the hairs of your head have all been
counted. So have no fear; you are worth more than
any number of sparrows.
MATTHEW 10.29–31 (NEB)

I remember a night some years ago with an exceptionally
hard frost. We have quite a few trees in our garden and of
course quite a number of birds, they roost in the branches.
What has stuck in my memory about that night is the inter-
mittent plop, plop, as one bird after another fell to the hard
ground, frozen to death. Now, was it by chance that some
sparrows fell and others did not? Or do we have to believe on
the basis of this saying of Jesus that the sparrow on one tree
fell frozen but not on the one next to it because God 'keeps
a tab' on all sparrows and follows a plan detailing which
sparrows should survive and which succumb? Similarly,
if God knows exactly how many hairs you have on your
head, he keeps a record, presumably knowing when an 'oldie'
among us goes bald. Surely we can't take this seriously! It is
an absurdity. So what was Jesus saying?

1 NOTHING TOO SMALL FOR GOD'S CONCERN

First of all, I think he was saying that there is nothing,
however small, however apparently insignificant, outside the
awareness of God. God is the Universal Presence, there is

nowhere where he is not. He is in fact the perpetual *sustainer* of all that is. Without that sustaining presence there would be no existence of anything at all. He is not simply the initial creator, he is the constant creator, that is to say he is always creating, always sustaining. This is why there is a world, why there is a natural order all about us.

To conceive of God like this is modern. In the fifteenth, sixteenth and seventeenth centuries science was getting into its stride and all manner of discoveries were being made about the world of nature. Telescopes, microscopes and many other devices for examining our environment were busy uncovering wonders. To the scientists who worked then nature appeared as some *wonderful machine* with a multitude of locking and interlocking units to keep it together and to keep it going. They were not Godless scientists, they believed in God, they believed God was the creator of all this, but having created this marvel there was nothing left for God to do. He could 'sit back', as it were, and let nature run itself, powered by its own momentum. Not surprisingly therefore, if God was not necessary for the machine, gradually they came to the conclusion that there was no point in believing in his existence at all. So little by little, in the face of the growing competence and self-assurance of science, God was dropped from the reckoning altogether.

But how do human beings fit into this picture? We aren't bits and pieces of one vast machine complex. We aren't predictable like the parts in the machine of a motor car. We have minds of our own, and individual desires and purposes, making us *un*predictable. So *the machine concept* of the world did not and will not hold, nor the idea that at some point in the dim and distant past God set it all going as we have it now. And this was, this is, the creation. All this mode of thinking had to be and was abandoned. We have to think of God differently from this, and the world differently, including of course what we mean by nature.

91

2 NATURE HAS A LIFE OF ITS OWN

Yes, God made the world, he continues to be making the world, which is why we have a world, but it does not function on a string on which he keeps a hold, it has a *life of its own*, it has an independence.

Come back then to those sparrows dropping off the trees dead because of the exceptionally hard frost that night. God was not sitting up in heaven knocking them down one by one. (Please forgive me for speaking so crudely, I only do so for the sake of trying to make difficult points clear.) The truth, surely, is that some sparrows dropped dead from the cold and others did not because the life forces in some birds were insufficiently stoked up by food to withstand the low temperature.

This is the point. Nature follows its own laws of cause and effect. So we must not attribute those terrible earthquakes and floods causing untold misery to the people trapped by them to the *direct* action of God. And we must not overthrow what belief we have in God because of those calamities. This is indeed God's world; he made it, he makes it, that is to say sustains it, but it is not under control like a motor car being driven along the highway, it is like a human being, restricted indeed by being human, but also free within the limits of being human.

So when Jesus said, 'Are not sparrows two a penny? Yet without your Father's leave not one of them can fall to the ground,' he was not talking nonsense. God has made a world where some sparrows will certainly fall to the ground when the temperature is excessively low. God knows, even down to such insignificant creatures as sparrows, priced at two a penny. God sees and God knows. But note what Jesus said, 'Not one of them can fall to the ground without *your Father's leave.*' He did not use the general word God, he called him 'your Father'. The God then who created all and sees all *cares about all*, like any good father watching over his family.

We must not therefore be satisfied to explain our world simply in terms of scientific abstraction. No, we must be aware of the all-seeing, all-caring heavenly Father. Jesus reinforced what he said about the sparrows by adding, 'As for you, even the hairs of your head have all been counted. So have no fear; you are worth more than any numbers of sparrows.' This is the message in all this *for us*.

3 GOD'S PURPOSES

And now something else arising out of what has been said so far. There is a purpose in God's creation. The creation does not exist simply for the sake of existing. And when we ask what that purpose is we can only answer in two words: 'for us'. The scientist, of course, will stop short of this. Purpose is not a category which scientific discipline will entertain, and understandably so. His task is to investigate and explain *what* is, not to attempt to suggest *why* it is. But we in the Church, with our belief in God, cannot stop there. And Jesus did not stop there. He brought the events of the world of nature, even apparently insignificant events like the falling of a sparrow to the ground, into connection with 'our Father'. We are asked to see events through the eyes of this faith, namely God the creator and sustainer as 'our Father'.

Can we then, dare we, go on from this and suggest that God sometimes uses events in the world for his purposes for specific people, groups of people like nations, and for individuals too? The Bible provides us with many examples, such as the deliverance of the Hebrew tribes from the slavery of Egypt and Saul of Tarsus deflected to the place of repentance and faith instead of persecuting the Christians as he intended. Were these merely coincidences, or was God at work?

May we then, dare we, believe that God makes some things happen *in our lives* because his purpose is behind them? They were not mere lucky breaks. When the couple come to be

93

married and say shyly, 'We were meant for each other,' is this all nonsense, or can we take providence seriously? When the great Augustine, St Augustine (354–430), on his voyage across the sea could not because of the gales land at Carthage, where he would immerse himself in Manichaeism, but was driven on to Rome, where he discovered and embraced the Christian faith, he believed this was God's purpose at work in a gale. Is this stupid? But I remember that profound Christian thinker Archbishop William Temple saying how he had discovered that when he was in periods of closest communion with God '*the coincidences*' occurred with greater frequency than at other times. But God, we must understand, does not exercise his control by interference, but by influence, and influence is something we can always reject. God's purposes are indeed a reality, but we are always left with our freedom, to accept or reject, to believe or disbelieve.

Please forgive me, the preacher, if a very modest personal testimony is out of place. I myself have good reason to believe in providence. I would never have exercised the ministry I came to exercise were it not for the apparently chance meeting of the young woman who became my wife (and has now died). In many ways she 'made' me.

Yes, I am bringing this vast subject of God the creator down to the personal level. But I am not wrong to do this when preaching on this striking saying of Jesus about the sparrows and the hairs of our heads. The great lessons are: first, nothing is too small for God's concern; second, nature has a life of its own; third, God's purposes are real. But all are brought into relationship with the *life we live*. Listen to the saying again: 'Are not sparrows two a penny? Yet without your Father's leave not one of them can fall to the ground. As for you, even the hairs of your head have all been counted. So have no fear; you are worth more than any number of sparrows.'

17
JESUS RELIGION

Come to me, all who labour and are heavy laden, and I will give you rest. Take my yoke upon you, and learn from me; for I am gentle and lowly in heart, and you will find rest for your souls. For my yoke is easy, and my burden is light.

MATTHEW 11.28–30 (RSV)

About a fortnight ago I watched the Sunday evening TV programme called *Songs of Praise*. Instead of the usual attendance at some particular church or chapel, on this occasion there was a presentation of a selection of the huge number of sacred songs and solos that drew audiences of many thousands to the evangelistic meetings where they could hear them and take part. This was in the last quarter of the nineteenth century, and the leaders were two Americans called Moody and Sankey. This BBC programme was excellently produced, and the two evangelists in particular were realistically and sensitively portrayed by two competent actors. There was a huge choir backed up by organ and instrumental music, and all the hymns, if they could be called hymns, had catchy and singable tunes with repetitive choruses, so catchy that I found myself all the following week singing them to myself or whistling the tunes.

Now if you press me I shall have to concede that there is very little depth in this type of religion, a minimum of theology and no obvious awareness of the outside world. It could be written off as shallow, but I do not want to write it off. It did a great work for ordinary and humble folk before and beyond the turn of the century. And it did have authentic Christian content, though admittedly very little. And it was not wholly subjective nor sheer emotionalism. It was firmly centred on Jesus, in coming to whom life of a new

95

quality was to be experienced. Take for example one of the refrains, 'I need thee, O I need thee, every hour I need thee, O cleanse me now my Saviour, I come to thee.' True, the doctrines of original sin and justification by faith were not elaborated, indeed hardly touched upon, but Jesus was made real and made relevant, a presentation that met people's need, elementary though it was, where they were, tired, anxious, sometimes merry, frequently sad and bewildered. And it touched on the certainty of a life beyond.

We may label this disparagingly as 'Jesus religion', but I ask you if it is not in alignment with the saying of Jesus himself in Matthew 11.28–30: 'Come to me, all who labour and are heavy laden, and I will give you rest. Take my yoke upon you, and learn from me; for I am gentle and lowly in heart, and you will find rest for your souls. For my yoke is easy, and my burden is light.'

1 CHRISTIANITY BEGINS WITH A STORY

Now you may say, it was all very well for Jesus to offer the invitation, 'Come to me,' but the Galileans whom he addressed could see him, indeed touch him, but how can we? He is beyond our sight and we cannot touch him. But he did live in this world, he was a real man, he is no legendary figure. He had to eat and drink and sleep just as we do, he knew the meaning of tiredness and was deeply moved by what he saw around him, both beauty and some of life's tragedies. This is the point I want to make, the Christian religion has its first elementary beginning when Jesus of Nazareth becomes a real person to us. And I want to add this, a Christian preacher is *fulfilling his calling* if he is able to make this Jesus a living reality so that the hearers feel they know him. I regret to have to say this, but it is true there have been, and are, some in the Christian ministry, learned men with famous names, who have no use for the gospels in the New Testament, and they are written off as mere stories.

96

For them Christianity begins with the writings of St Paul. Now I would be the last person to underrate the great apostle, but I have to say that for most ordinary men and women, to begin with at any rate, he is far too difficult, far too theological. What people need first of all is a person able to be seen and heard, even if the two words have to be in inverted commas. This means presenting the historical Jesus as he was, and the gospels standing there at the beginning of the New Testament enable this to be done. And unless it is done the words of my text today will not make sense. 'Come to me, all who labour and are heavy laden.' We cannot *come to* a theory first of all, we can only come to a person. I contend, therefore, though some would disagree with me, that telling the story of Jesus *is preaching the gospel*, at least at its beginning. It is not possible to be a Christian without knowing about Jesus, though knowing about Jesus is not in itself Christianity, but this is where it begins. It begins with a story about a person. So Moody and Sankey were not wrong in their approach captured in the words of one of their best-known choruses, 'Tell me the old, old story of Jesus and his love.'

2 THE PEOPLE ADDRESSED

We return to the text. 'Come to me, all who labour and are heavy laden.' Whom did Jesus invite to come to him? The answer is plain, 'all who labour and are heavy laden'. This meant the broad mass of people who lived in Palestine. Endless toil was their lot. There were some rich people who lived off their property in the form of estates, but very very few. There was no middle class, everyone was dependent on their own labour, mainly the labour of their own hands. In the main they were an agricultural people living off the crops they produced. Stock-breeding was another dominant occupation, mainly sheep and goats. The herds were enormous, a man might be in charge of ten thousand sheep;

97

the labour involved is almost unthinkable. Then there was fishing, especially on the shore of the Lake of Galilee teeming with fish. These men were held in high regard and formed clubs, rather like trade unions. Life in Palestine depended on their catches, there could be no release from this daily and nightly toil. In addition to these predominant occupations there were potters who made the cooking utensils, carpenters for the building and care of the tiny houses and for making and repairing the ploughs for the workers on the land and yokes and other pieces of equipment for the stock-breeders. There was in addition a tiny group which did not labour with their hands, the tax-gatherers and the money-lenders counted in the community as above the ordinary, and there were the scribes who had built up for themselves a monopoly of interpreting the law and were generally thought of, not least by themselves, as definitely superior, a class apart.

All this means that we are not to think of Jesus offering his invitation to only one class, the labouring class. It was addressed to everybody. He did not even exclude the tax-gatherers, who were generally hated by the community as a whole, indeed he went out of his way on one occasion to call one named Levi as a kind of public demonstration of the wide scope of his approach. The best response to his invitation, however, seems to have come from the more successful and competent traders, men who could read and write some Greek and so engage in the general commerce where a knowledge of the language was essential. They were a cut above the general run of the people educationally, with a capacity to learn. It would seem that Jesus recruited his disciples from these traders who lived near or close to the northern shores of the Lake of Galilee. The scribes were different. They belonged to Jerusalem and its neighbourhood and were hostile to Jesus' invitation because it undercut their privileged profession. They were not loved in the community and not trusted, because they laid, or tried to lay, impossible religious burdens on people, and that with an arrogant and demanding, attitude, flaunting their superiority. There were

613 rules and regulations to be obeyed in their system, an impossible load for ordinary people.

3 THE INVITATION OF JESUS

Once we have understood what life was like when Jesus lived in Judaea and Galilee we begin to understand the strength of Jesus' appeal. First of all, this invitation was for every-body, there were no limits. Not even those money-grubbing tax-gatherers, publicans, as they were called, were left out. And what about the scribes? Let me read you some verses from St Mark's gospel (which Matthew included in his gospel):

> And one of the scribes came up and heard them disputing with one another, and seeing that he answered them well, asked him, 'Which commandment is the first of all?' Jesus answered, 'The first is, "Hear, O Israel: The Lord our God, the Lord is one; and you shall love the Lord your God with all your heart, and with all your soul, and with all your mind, and with all your strength." The second is this, "You shall love your neighbour as yourself." There is no other commandment greater than these.' And the scribe said to him, 'You are right, Teacher; you have truly said that he is one, and there is no other but he; and to love him with all the heart, and with all the understanding, and with all the strength, and to love one's neighbour as oneself, is much more than all whole burnt offerings and sacrifices.' And when Jesus saw that he answered wisely, he said to him, 'You are not far from the kingdom of God.'
>
> (Mark 12.28–34, RSV)

This is astonishing, quite astonishing. A scribe of all people simplifying the immense clutter of his religious system into one commandment of love of God and love of neighbour. Jesus must have been astonished, but it gives us a clear indication of wherein lay the strength of Jesus' appeal, not only its universality but its simplicity. No wonder he said, 'Take my yoke upon you, and learn from me . . . For my yoke is easy, and my burden is light.' The religion of Jesus made its claims. There was a yoke to be borne, but it was easy and light in comparison with what the scribes laid on people (but there was at least that one exception). The stock-breeders, the tillers of the soil, the fishermen, the potters and the carpenters must have groaned under what was expected of them religiously; it was impossible, their lives were too full of trial and burdens already, they couldn't take any more. And then Jesus came along proclaiming his simplified view of religion summed up in that remarkable saying set down in Matthew 7.12, 'So whatever you wish that men would do to you, do so to them; *for this is the law and the prophets.*' They must have wondered if they were hearing aright. It was so simple, so straightforward, so general and universal in its approach. Ordinary people could take that, yes, even me, especially those who labour and are heavy laden. Jesus and his message really was for them.

4 JESUS' YOKE

We are not to think that his message contained no demands on his hearers at all. They had to take his yoke upon them. Some of them would probably have made yokes in the local carpenters' shops. It was a wooden device which enabled the oxen to work side by side, sharing the burden of pulling the load or ploughing the field. Perhaps Jesus had actually made yokes himself, he had worked as a carpenter in all probability and no doubt made well-fitting comfortable yokes; perhaps his father's and his shop was noted for them. The people who lived in Nazareth and round about would know this. When therefore he said, 'Take my yoke upon you, and learn from me; for I am gentle and lowly in heart, and you will find rest for your souls. For my yoke is easy, and my burden is light', the words would come alive. And what was the yoke? It is compressed into one sentence, another of the memorable sayings of Jesus, perhaps the most memorable of them all: 'So whatever you wish that men would do to you, do so to them; for this is the law and the prophets.'

This was new, completely new. Something like it, it is true, formed a plank in various ethical systems, not least that of the scribes in Judaism, but there was this big difference. They all counselled, 'What you would not like men to do to you, don't do to them.' We can imagine a boy in a family tearing at his young brother's hair, and his mother stopping him. 'Don't do that Johnny, you would not like him to do it to you.' The negative was given as the spring of action here, as in ethical systems generally, but not in Jesus' teaching. His way was positive. It was, 'Whatever you wish that man would do to you, do so to him.' This was a call to positive good-ness to our fellow men and women, not simply a call to refrain from positive badness. This was the yoke, Jesus' yoke, a requirement to go out of our way to be a positive benefit to people.

Did Jesus' hearers take this in? They saw the help he himself gave to the blind, the deaf, the crippled, the diseased, and those whom society rejected like the tax-gatherers. He did for them what he would like them to do for him if their positions were reversed. And so his message, 'Come to me, and learn from me.'

I find this challenging. I wonder how ready I am to go out of my way to help individuals I encounter in need. It was a bother to stop the car the other day and give that poor woman a lift, partly crippled and stumbling along with her heavy shopping. But if I were in her shoes I would like her to do that for me. O so simple an illustration, but if this is the kind of action 'Jesus religion' entails, I will not be one to despise its simplicity. It may lack theological depth, but if our Christianity does not begin and continue here it has not even begun to learn of Christ. This is the rub in 'the old, old story of Jesus and his love'.

18

BAD LANGUAGE, GOOD LANGUAGE

You can tell a tree by its fruit.
MATTHEW 12.33 (NEB)

Here is a young man of about twenty-eight, a clergyman. He has been an assistant curate for five years and now is appointed to 'a living' as it is called. He is married and there is a vicarage into which they must move, a house with a garden. They don't know much about gardening but they will have to learn because they will have to keep it. They first see the place in winter and happen to notice that there are four or five trees in the garden, but what they are they have no idea. In the autumn, however, they do know, because one, trained up against the south wall of the house, produced the most lovely William pears, another eating apples and another cooking apples. They knew then what the trees were, for as my text for this sermon, one of the sayings of Jesus, has it, 'You can tell a tree by its fruit.'

1 UNGUARDED SPEECH

Now the meaning of this saying seems obvious, what more is there to say? We need to notice, however, when Jesus uttered it, and all three of the first three gospels, the synoptic gospels as they are called, record it. So it was important in the mind of Jesus. 'You can tell a tree by its fruit.' This was said when some people, clearly caring people, brought him a wretched man whose mental balance was so damaged that he was both blind and dumb. And Jesus cured him, restoring both sight and speech. Not surprisingly those who witnessed this dramatic healing were amazed and began to enquire of one another if this healer could possibly be the Messiah. When however the Pharisees overheard what was being suggested they reacted with hostility. No! This man, this Jesus, is in league with the devil; what we see here is Satanic power operating in our very midst.

Did the Pharisees really believe this? How could they? The devil does not build people up, but rather beats them down. Or were these Pharisees simply employing 'any old argument' because they were put out by this stranger performing wonderful works which thrilled the people, drawing all their attention? Or was it that this was merely an unthinking comment on their part, words 'off the cuff' as we say, an unreflective outburst of feeling? Whatever it was, Jesus took it seriously because what people say is an index of what those people are. 'You can tell a tree by its fruit'.

Modern psychology is aware of this. Careful note is taken of what a man or woman says in *unguarded* moments. It is the asides that are most revealing, not the set speeches when someone is known to be listening. This does not mean we can write off the speeches on the floor of the House of Commons, they have been carefully prepared and carefully uttered, but if you wish to know what is the real character of the speaker, oh! that is different, you listen to him in the tea room when he is simply chatting. What people say is an index of what they are. 'You can tell a tree by its fruit.'

2 BAD LANGUAGE

This matter of how we speak is not a side issue in modern Britain; it never was of course. I am not referring to regional dialect, nor to ungrammatical speech, but to what is commonly known as 'bad language'. This has spread enormously in recent years, not least on television. If then the saying of Jesus is true, 'You can tell a tree by its fruit,' this modern slide into bad language and the widespread and ready acceptance of it is an index of the modern slide into character decline in the community at large.

Now I am well aware that the use of what are called 'swear words' is due on the part of the uneducated and illiterate primarily to ignorance of what words to employ when he/she wishes to emphasize what he/she has to say. Basically it is little more than that. When such a person describes something as 'bloody good' he is simply wanting to say that it is exceedingly good, but such words would be completely foreign to him, and even open to ridicule from his associates. We ought not therefore to take this kind of bad language too seriously. But what are we to think of the reasonably educated person who constantly interpolates his talk with 'swear words'? Here is a visit being paid to a patient in hospital by a doctor after an operation which deprived the patient of sleep day and night for an entire week. At last, however, he could remove the apparatus which prohibited rest. 'Now', said the doctor, 'you will be able to get a bloody good sleep.' He meant it kindly, but what did his words say about him? That he was a caring practitioner? Maybe. 'You can tell a tree by its fruit.'

3 BLASPHEMY

I pass now to blasphemy. The third of the ten commandments deals with this. 'Thou shalt not take the name of the Lord thy God in vain; for the Lord will not hold him guiltless that taketh his name in vain.' Taking a name 'in vain' means making an empty use of it. Maybe we are surprised that this misuse of language with reference to God should have its place alongside such clearly culpable actions as murder, adultery and stealing, but the inference is obvious. Blasphemy is a serious offence which will not be without consequences. In the long run it will bring about the ruination of civilization. We need to be careful. Christians need to be especially careful how freely and thoughtlessly they interject the word 'Christ!'

when something surprises them and perhaps hurts them. It is to be wondered if people who use the name of the Saviour in this loose way really are Christians or only imitation. 'You can tell a tree by its fruit.' Let me put it to you. What would you think of the man and his relation to his wife if he dragged her name in simply to emphasize his displeasure or surprise at something that was happening to him? You would wonder how much, or rather how little, he really loved her.

4 UNFORGIVABLE SLANDER

And now we turn once more to the context where this saying of Jesus occurs. 'You can tell a tree by its fruit.' Let me quote the words of Jesus which are part of that context. 'And so I tell you this: no sin, no slander, is beyond forgiveness for men, except slander spoken against the Spirit, and that will not be forgiven. Any man who speaks a word against the Son of Man will be forgiven; but if anyone speaks against the Holy Spirit, for him there is no forgiveness, either in this age or in the age to come.'

What are we to make of this? What is slander spoken against the Holy Spirit? I think we have to go back again to the occasion when Jesus said this. It was when he had cured a wretched man who was both blind and dumb. The people who witnessed this were amazed and showed their amazement by what they said, 'Can this be the Son of David?' But what about the Pharisees who said, 'This is the devil's work.' Did they believe what they were saying? Surely not. What they were doing was deliberately calling good evil for their own nefarious purposes. This is bad. It is purposely confusing moral distinctions. It is harbouring a lie in the soul, and sooner or later it destroys the faculty by which the difference between good and evil can be distinguished. No matter if forgiveness is offered to such slanderers, *they cannot receive it* because the faculty for even appreciating the difference is no more.

105

5 GOOD LANGUAGE

We have been thinking about bad language. Perhaps you count this a trivial matter, and it very often is, the product of ignorance or slovenliness. Could we then give our attention to the converse, that is good language. Surely the Christian ought to employ this, but what is it? What is good language? Certainly not speech interlarded at every possible point with biblical texts. To encounter this at its worst we need to acquaint ourselves with Puritans of the fifteenth century. But this kind of speech is not good language, it is artificial language, it is 'put on' as we say, it seeks to bamboozle telling what the 'tree is by its fruit'. Good speech is natural speech. It issues from what the speaker is. 'You can tell a tree by its fruit.' Out 'of the abundance of the heart his mouth speaketh' (Luke 6.45).

And in all this the manner and tone of voice of the speaker are important. Learn a lesson from your dog. He does not understand your words, or very few anyway, but he knows what you are saying, judging by the sound of your voice and manner in addressing him. Anger and kindliness are recognized at once. We humans could learn from this. The way we speak is important, the tone of voice, the look in the eye, and the expression on the face. Good speech, good language, always respects the people being addressed. It does not beat down. It does not treat the hearers as inferior, using conversation to belittle them. Listen to the man or woman addressing a titled person and the same person addressing the refuse collector. It will tell you much about that person.

There is a proper Christian way to talk, and it is not pious, artificial or solemn. It is ready for a laugh and shows an interest in ordinary people and ordinary affairs. And of course the language is always sincere and not devious. The Christian does not, like Talleyrand, use words to hide his meaning and not disclose it. And it must be clear, straightforward and concise, not like Oliver Cromwell, a great man in many respects, but who could not refrain from so complicating what he had to say that the hearer had no idea what he meant.

Come back to my text. 'You can tell a tree by its fruit.' How alarming, how hard this apparently simple saying of Jesus turns out to be. But then, much of what Jesus said is hard.

19

A RICH FOOL

Man, who made me a judge or divider over you?
LUKE 12.14 (RSV)

The New English Bible has backed down on what Jesus actually said. Perhaps we would like to back down too. The NEB reads, '*My good man*, who set me over you to judge or arbitrate?' The substituted phrase 'My good man' is gentle in comparison. We find it hard to believe that Jesus would be so brusque with the curt 'Man!' But we had better be wary about deciding what Jesus must have said and altering what he did actually say as the Greek original in Luke 12.14 has it. It was indeed blunt. Clearly Jesus was deliberately putting a gap between this man and himself. He was distancing himself. Apparently he was ready to do this if need be. He was not a perpetually soft and accommodating person. He could push people away and keep them at 'arms length'. So this intruder on Jesus' teaching of the crowds one day experienced his cold shoulder.

1 HOW RELIGION MUST NOT BE USED

Does this surprise us? Even upset us? We had better visualize the scene. A man in the crowd called out to Jesus, 'Master, tell my brother to divide the family property with me.' Jesus did not yield an inch. Instead this blunt refusal, 'Man, who made me a judge or divider over you?' What was at issue here? It was that this intruder on Jesus' discourse was attempting to make use of Jesus for his own ends. Never mind whether he had a legitimate case against his brother or not, Jesus wasn't interested. He was not in the business of financial arbitration and settling property rights. He was certainly not going to help one brother gain ascendancy over the other, whatever the rights or wrongs of the situation, by alleging that he had Jesus on his side.

This is the point. Religion is not to be employed as a makeweight in our mundane affairs. Perhaps there is a warning here for politicians. It can be tempting to adopt the high moral ground, not because it is fervently believed in but because it might win votes. We can be sure Christ distances himself from all political disagreements and party strife. He is not in that business. This does not mean politicians must have no religious convictions, but they must not employ them to score points over the other side. To Tory, Labour and Liberal Democrat, Jesus would say, 'Man, who made me a judge or divider over you?'

2 THE DANGER FOR THE RICH MAN

Come back now to the actual incident. Having been rebuked, the seeker after Jesus' support in a family quarrel (if such it was) faded into the background, no doubt a little sore at the cold shouldering he had received, and Jesus continued with his preaching to the crowds. But his sternness continued: 'Beware,' he said. 'Be on your guard against greed of every kind' – so is this what Jesus sensed in the man who interrupted him? – for even when a man has more than enough, his wealth does not give him life.' Most people find this hard to believe. With a win on 'the pools' life would be wonderful. Would it? Perhaps at first, possibly, but after a few weeks? Make no mistake, Jesus was not opposed to possessions. He did not condemn riches outright, nor did he thrust the rich man out beyond the pale. But every rich man has a problem. He is liable to be dominated by his riches. Far from a release into freedom, he may be thrust into a bondage he had never thought of. He is liable never to be contented. He wants more and more. And not only that, he is dogged by worries that he might lose what he has. How then will he manage? He has become tied to a certain lifestyle. So insurance becomes a prime concern. The rich man has by then become a bondsman to his wealth, a prisoner in fact, and a prisoner is never a happy man. Moreover, riches can very easily lend to the personality a certain superiority or hauteur which is isolating. Were the words of Jesus too strong then? 'Beware,' he said, 'be on your guard against greed of every kind, for even when a man has more than enough, his wealth does not give him life.' So what about the National Lottery?

For some years I had a secretary (she died a few years ago) who, being 'well-provided for' as the saying goes, did not require any wages, she worked for me in the Christian ministry for nothing. She was 'well-connected' (as they say), and one of the phrases she used to describe some friend or associate of hers, and which stuck in my mind, was 'Poor little rich girl.' Had she seen for herself that wealth does not necessarily bring happiness?

Come back again to Jesus' words. 'Even when a man has more than enough, his wealth does not give him life.' The crucial phrase here is 'more than enough'. What the rich man, if he wishes to experience life, has to decide is *when he has enough*. It isn't easy. He can easily deceive himself, but his happiness depends on making this decision and acting upon it. He must decide what to do with that money and to know that the worst possible conclusion would be to use it all for himself. This is the way to enlarge self-centredness, and self-centredness is the sure road to discontentment. He must give his excess away, employ it to assist good causes, or engage in relief work of some kind for no pay whatsoever. There are men and women who have done this. There are Christian rich people and they are happy – you can tell by their faces.

110

3 WHEN A RICH MAN IS A FOOL

Come back once again to the incident in which this blunt
retort which I took as my text is set. Let me read it to you.
'And he told them this parable: "There was a rich man
whose land yielded heavy crops. He debated with himself:
'What am I to do? I have not the space to store my produce.
This is what I will do,' said he: 'I will pull down my storehouses and build them bigger. I will collect in them all my
corn and other goods.'"' Well, what is wrong with that?
Surely what he decided was common sense. It would be
stupid to leave his ample produce out in all weathers to rot,
and his other goods too. Certainly build larger storehouses.
Why not? But here comes his mistake, when he had done
this he decided he would say to himself, 'Man, you have
plenty of good things laid by, enough for many years: take
life easy, eat, drink, and enjoy yourself.' That is to say, he
decided to set himself in the centre of his life in the future;
work would be no longer necessary, he had barns full of
produce. Well, what is wrong with that? Don't we all ease up
a bit when we come to the time of retirement? No longer
that wearisome drive morning and evening, backwards and
forwards to the big city; no longer that scramble to be in
time at the station to catch that businessman's train. Yes, but
the danger is that we shall turn our attention on ourselves.
All our attention will be on what I want and what I can now
have. And that is the way to become a small man, a small
woman, someone with limited vision, a person unable to
appreciate anything beyond the near and the personal,
indeed to experience a shrinkage of soul.

And now the shock interruption to this man's ruminations.
Two words: 'But God'. He had forgotten about God. He
reckoned he himself had organized his life and his business
pretty well. Weren't his storehouses 'chock-a-block' with
goods? But God had better not be forgotten. Our lives are in
his hands, whether we are aware of the fact or not, and he,

not ourselves, will have the last word. But God said to him, 'Fool.' Yes, I looked up the word in the Greek. It is not the kindly word that Jesus used to reprove his disciples on the road to Emmaus after his resurrection, 'O foolish men, and slow of heart to believe all that the prophets have spoken' (Luke 24.25, RSV). Here in the parable which Jesus told, the word is stark, rough and wounding, 'Fool, this very night you must surrender your life.' However successful you appear to have ordered your life, don't forget God will have the last word. 'You have made your money – who will get it now?' End of parable, but Jesus had one comment to make after the fall of the curtain. 'That is how it is with the man who amasses wealth for himself and remains a pauper in the sight of God.'

*   *   *

So Mr Rich Man, so Madam, Rich Woman, you are not wrong to make a success of your business, and to own property, but be careful not to put yourself in the centre of your picture, you will not be happy. What is more, if you leave God out of your reckoning altogether, you will be a fool. For of this you can be sure, God will have the last word with you; yes and with me, and with all of us, whether we have larger storehouses crammed with produce or not. The real wisdom is to reckon that whatever happens we are in God's hands.

20

A HARD SAYING

Do you think that I have come to give peace on earth?
No, I tell you, but rather division.
LUKE 12.51 (RSV)

Some months ago a relative of mine heard that I was writing
a book on the sayings of Jesus. When I met him he raised
the subject and said provokingly, 'What will you do with
this one: "Do you think that I have come to give peace on
earth? No, I tell you, but rather division"?' It certainly is a
hard saying, and the temptation is to dodge it. For a start, it
appears to be in flat contradiction to one of our basic beliefs
about Christ. He is the 'Prince of Peace'. Do not the words
of Isaiah we hear at Christmas ring in our ears? 'For unto us
a child is born, unto us a son is given: and the government
shall be upon his shoulder: and his name shall be called
Wonderful, Counseller, The mighty God, The everlasting
Father, The Prince of Peace. Of the increase of his government and peace there shall be no end.' Indeed with the
music of Handel's *Messiah* in our ears we can scarcely stop
singing it. 'Prince of Peace'! Marvellous! And then this:
'There were shepherds out in the field, keeping watch over
their flocks by night, and a multitude of the heavenly host
praising God and saying, "Glory to God in the highest, and
on earth peace, among men with whom he is pleased."' And
as if that were not enough to establish Christ's name with
peace, in the fourth gospel we read that the night before his
death he said to his disciples, 'Peace I leave with you, my
peace I give unto you. Let not your hearts be troubled.' We
warm to these peaceful sayings. They are music to our ears.
What then is this hard, dissonant sentence on the very lips
of Jesus himself: 'Do you think that I have come to give

113

peace on earth? No, I tell you, but rather division.' Did he really say this? If so, it is a hard saying all-right. What are we to do with it? Dodge it? Reject it as unauthentic? It is not surprising that my relative should ask, 'What will you do with it?' This is the burden of my sermon today.

1 CHRIST'S PEACE COSTS

First of all this hard saying places an explosive charge underneath rosy interpretations of what Christianity is. Jesus was not rosy and Christ was not, is not, a magician. He came nowhere near waving a wand over the world to make it settle down into peaceful harmony. Peace indeed is what he came to bring; peace in human relationships, peace in the human heart, peace about the unknown future. But it would involve struggle, sometimes desperate, very often costly. 'My peace I leave with you,' said Jesus to his disciples in the Upper Room on what we have come to call Maundy Thursday, knowing that in a matter of hours he would be writhing in agony on a cross, the most diabolical form of execution ever invented. No, there is nothing smooth about Christ's peace, nothing cheap, nothing easy, nothing automatic. Christ's peace costs. This is the first lesson to draw from this hard saying, 'Do you think that I have come to give peace on earth? No, I tell you, but rather division.'

2 CHRIST IS A DIVISIVE FIGURE

And this leads directly into the second lesson to be drawn from this hard saying which we may wish to avoid but cannot, Christ is a *divisive figure*.

Jesus was not a jolly man. He was not a funny man. He was not a 'hail-fellow-well-met' type. But this in no way means that he was a man to be avoided. His company was sought, he was invited to social occasions, easily crossing social barriers. The crowds were fascinated by him, his closest followers adored him, humble men for the most part, but women too, supporting him with gifts in their normal feminine way. But he was not easy to understand. Kindly, caring and compassionate, certainly, and never overbearing, yet standing apart; the sort people thought twice about before approaching, the sort the superficial could not, cannot, tolerate. On these grounds alone Jesus was a divisive figure, and in time the divisions of opinion about him took on sharp hostile attitudes. He was even called a devil and a madman. And this strife in the community about him was evident to Jesus himself. So there came a day when he met it head on with this saying, 'Do you think that I have come to give peace on earth? No, I tell you, but rather division.' Clearly he was, he is, a divisive figure, one for whom we may be for or against. Evangelicals are not therefore wrong when in their evangelistic campaigns they call upon their hearers to 'decide for Christ'. Jesus was at the furthest possible remove from being a colourless figure. In meeting him people automatically found themselves deciding for or against. Christ is, I repeat, a divisive figure. There is no escaping this. It is a basic fact.

3 REPENTANCE IS INVOLVED

A third lesson to be learned from this hard saying is that to decide for Christ calls for a change of mind, a change of attitude not only to him but also to oneself. This means repentance. Let us be open about this. We do not like repenting. No one does. It hurts our pride. And even if in a measure we manage it, we are ready with our excuses for the kind of people we have become. Our genes, our family background, the community in which we have to work, our desperate shortage of money, our wretched housing. We know it all, and trot it out to excuse those things in our conduct we have to admit do not begin to square with the conduct that could even in the broadest sense be counted as Christian. So it costs to decide for Christ. It always has and it always will. The price is repentance – *metanoia*, to use the New Testament Greek word, meaning basically 'to change the mind' – and we don't like doing it. We can't however get away from repentance if we associate with Christianity at all, even in the broadest form of Christian worship on occasions. It always begins with a confession. If not in the old words of the Prayer Book, 'We have erred and strayed from thy ways like lost sheep . . . we have left undone those things we ought to have done, and we have done those things which we ought not to have done,' then in more modern language, but making that same admission of falling far short of the way God would have us live. And it hurts our pride. We don't like stepping down from our platform of self-justification. I say 'we', for I include myself, the ordained preacher.

And this is the point I have to hammer home, repentance is the essential prelude to peace, the peace Christ comes to bring. There can't be peace, Christian peace, without repentance, and the price is humility. And I tell you this, men and women who are ready to acknowledge and repent of their own shortfalls are far, far less likely to be troublemakers in the community in which they live than the self-righteous and arrogant, they will in fact in a troubled world actually make for peace. It will be Christ's peace, the peace he came to bring.

4 CHRISTIAN PEACE INVOLVES LOVE

And now, fourthly, what is Christian peace, the peace which is costly, involves repentance and is rooted in decision for Christ? It is certainly much more than absence of hostility, or in worldly terms a laying down of arms; this is but the bare negative aspect. In Christian peace there is indeed no more sniping, no more revenge taking, no more trap laying, no more rejoicing in another's downfall, but there is more than this. Christian peace is positive, it fills the vacuum after the clatter of conflict has ceased. It is in fact love of other people, people from whom we differ, differ in temperament, in dialect, in style and maybe intellectually; even, dare I say it, but Christ said it, love of enemies. Christian peace is at bottom love of people, an acquired cultivated attitude come by and through the grace of God. Love is the epitome of the Spirit of Christ, indeed it is the outflowing of his Spirit. Listen to Paul, writing to that faction-ridden church in Galatia: 'The fruit of the Spirit is love, joy, peace, patience, kindness, goodness, fidelity, gentleness, and self-control.' Christian peace is all so much more than the mere cessation of hostilities.

*   *   *

And now I come back to where I began, indeed to that hard saying of Jesus, 'Do you think that I have come to give peace on earth? No, I tell you, but rather division.' Christ's peace is not an easy ride. Because it is the consequence of a decision for Christ, it may be divisive. Some are for Christ, others are against Christ. It has always been so. And the resulting divisions may extend even to the most natural and intimate relationships. Let me complete the hard saying of Jesus as we have it in Luke 12.51: 'Do you think that I have come to give peace on earth? No, I tell you, but rather division; for henceforth in one house there will be five divided, three against two and two against three; they will be divided, father against son and son against father, mother against daughter and daughter against her mother, mother-in-law against her daughter-in-law and daughter-in-law against her mother-in-law.' Such can be, not 'must be', the outcome of decision for Christ on the part of some members of the family and not others. We regret it deeply, but there it is.

Here is a true and recent story about a Muslim family. The father wrote to his son telling him that he was standing out like a thorn. Over a period of ten years he had spent time

117

and money in nourishing his boy in the Islamic faith and he was the only one of six children who had forsaken it. He said he was ready to take the boy back, but if he remained a Christian he must understand that he could no longer count him as father. The boy made his choice and was completely and utterly cut off from his family. This is what his new found faith cost him.

An extreme case of deciding for Christ and his peace, though not in some parts of the world? But tensions in family circles are always possible because of the demands the faith entails. We had better not discard this hard saying of Jesus, 'Do you think that I have come to give peace on earth? No, I tell you, but rather division.' We must face the truth. Christ brings peace, but it costs.

21
RELIGIOUS PRIDE

For every one who exalts himself will be humbled, and he who humbles himself will be exalted.
LUKE 14.11 (RSV)

It is not possible to get away from this saying of Jesus, it occurs three times in the synoptic gospels, each in a different context. Clearly it was a statement Jesus repeated again and again, but it would seem from the three occurrences in St Matthew and St Luke that it was always with the Pharisees distinctly in mind. It was not a statement about people in general, which is not to say it has no universal application, but originally on the lips of Jesus it was a deliberate attack on the Pharisees of his day.

Who were the Pharisees? They were the dominant religious influence in the land. As a party they had come into existence rather more than a hundred years before the time of Christ in opposition to the policies of the Maccabean rulers. Their aim was to establish a pure religious Judaism with an emphasis on obedience in every department of life to the Jewish cere-monial system. The word Pharisees means 'separated ones'. They were the puritans of their time. They were bitterly opposed to Jesus, and he found himself in open conflict with them on many occasions. The people in general recognized their leadership with lip service while counting their religious requirement an impossible burden. The tax-gatherers, of course, were outside the pale altogether. Let us turn then to consider the three occasions when Jesus uttered this polemical saying, 'For every one who exalts himself will be humbled, and he who humbles himself will be exalted.'

1 THE SCRAMBLE FOR CHIEF SEATS

First we have to try and imagine a smart house with a smart dinner-table laid, the entire scene an utter contrast to the humble dwelling places of the Galilean folk Jesus knew so well. It was a sabbath day and Jesus was a guest invited by the host, a man who occupied a ruling position in the community and who belonged to the Pharisees. Some other Pharisees were also guests, and so blatant were their attentions fixed on Jesus, everything he did and everything he said, that plainly this was not a straightforward social occasion. Jesus had been invited into a trap. Then it happened. A man infected with dropsy appeared in the room (as was possible in the open house planning of the time), and presented himself before Jesus, obviously looking for healing. This was a gift for the Pharisaic host and the other guests, a trap which had conveniently laid itself on. Jesus, however, did not wait to be caught, he took the lead. Fixing his eyes on the lawyers (yes, the host had made sure lawyers were there), and fixing his eyes too on the Pharisees who were doggedly noting his every word and movement, Jesus asked a general question, 'Is it lawful to heal on the sabbath, or not?' There was dead silence. The Pharisees were not to be trapped. So Jesus deliberately healed the man and let him go. Then turning back to the tongue-tied and embarrassed Pharisees, he put his second question: 'Which of you, having an ass or an ox that has fallen into a well, will not immediately pull him out on a sabbath day?' No answer. But Jesus had not finished. He had been watching the scramble for the best seats on the part of the guests before the meal began, that is, the positions of honour, and this is what he said, 'When you are invited by any one to a marriage feast, do not sit down in a place of honour, lest a more eminent man than you be invited by him; and he who invited you both will come and say to you, "Give place to this man," and then you will begin with shame to take the lowest place . . . For every one who exalts himself will be humbled, and he who humbles himself will be exalted.' Did the Pharisees present smart under this subtle criticism of their social behaviour, they in their ostentatious clothing and Jesus in his peasant's garb? There was more to come. It had not been a comfortable dinner party. That saying stuck in their gullet. 'Everyone who exalts himself will be humbled.' No wonder they hated this Jesus. He embarrassed them.

2 A PHARISEE PRAYING AND A TAX-GATHERER PRAYING

And now a different kind of scene altogether (Luke 18.9–14). Two men walking side by side on their way up to the Temple to pray. An odd pair, but they had nothing to do with each other, they just happened to meet, as it were, on the way to church. One was a Pharisee and the other a tax-gatherer. Could two people have been further apart? At the entrance they parted, the Pharisee proceeding to the front in a conspicuous position, the taxman swerving off to the side and back. The Pharisee, of course, intended to be seen. He would be showing any bystanders who might be present how they should observe the Jewish rules about the frequency of prayer. He stood to pray. Everyone would see him up at the front. Perhaps it was a Monday or a Thursday, the shopping days when more people would be about. The Pharisee's mind was on them. And this was his prayer, which wasn't in fact a prayer at all, for he asked God for nothing. He began, 'God, I thank thee that I am not like other men' – separation then in his first breath! – 'extortioners, unjust, adulterers' – and then with a glance to the back of the building – 'or even like this tax collector' – they had walked up together – 'I fast twice a week, I give tithes of all that I get' – a real Pharisee then, pressing home the minutiae of the Jewish ceremonial law – end of prayer! In complete contrast, the taxman kept his eyes on the ground, but unlike the

Pharisee he did actually pray, standing there inconspicuously, 'God, be merciful to me a sinner!' Moreover, he beat his breast. I don't know if Jesus saw this little drama take place, but he turned it into a parable and told it, according to St Luke, face to face to the Pharisees themselves, who trusted in themselves that they were righteous and despised others. 'I tell you,' he said when he had finished describing what had taken place, 'this man [the tax man] went down to his house justified rather than the other [the Pharisee]; for every one who exalts himself will be humbled, but he who humbles himself will be exalted.' So the taxman was placed high above the Pharisee. Could anything be more galling to the Pharisees? A taxman declared to be superior to them, the religious leaders!

3 A STINGING VERBAL ASSAULT

And now the third incident (Matthew 23), Jesus scraping the barrel to find words biting enough to hurl at the Pharisees, and all this only days before he was crucified. First he addressed the crowds and his disciples before proceeding to a direct assault on the scribes (i.e. lawyers) and the Pharisees. 'The scribes and the Pharisees', he said, 'sit on Moses' seat; so practise and observe whatever they tell you, but not what they do; for they preach, but do not practise. They bind heavy burdens, hard to bear, and lay them on men's shoulders; but they themselves will not move them with their finger. They do all their deeds to be seen by men; for they make their phylacteries broad and their fringes long [parts of their special religious attire], and they love the place of honour at feasts and the best seats in the synagogues, and salutations in the market places, and being called rabbi by men.' And then, turning to the scribes and Pharisees face to face, this famous saying: 'Whoever exalts himself will be humbled, and whoever humbles himself will be exalted.'

We can scarcely believe our ears. Did Jesus really speak in this fashion?

'Woe to you, scribes and Pharisees, hypocrites! . . . you traverse sea and land to make a single proselyte, and when he becomes a proselyte, you make him twice as much a child of hell as yourselves . . . Woe to you, blind guides, who say, "If any one swears by the temple, it is nothing; but if any one swears by the gold of the temple, he is bound by his oath." You blind fools! For which is greater, the gold or the temple that has made the gold sacred? . . . Woe to you, scribes and Pharisees, hypocrites! for you tithe mint and dill and cummin, and have neglected the weightier matters of the law, justice and mercy and faith . . . Woe to you, scribes and Pharisees, hypocrites! for you cleanse the outside of the cup and of the plate, but inside they are full of extortion and rapacity . . . You serpents, you brood of vipers, how are you to escape being sentenced to hell?'

4 THE LESSON FOR US

What are we to learn from this? Surely that Jesus condemned pride in no uncertain terms. Pride is no rarity. There are people so proud of their pedigree they despise those they label 'the commonfolk'. They are not pleasant to meet. There are people proud of the achievements, which are not to be denied, people proud of their family, people proud of their wealth, people proud of their looks. We may wish to argue that there is such a disposition as a proper pride, and who will deny it? I have heard it said of someone, as you must, 'The trouble is he has no pride in his work.' Or of a scruffy young man applying for a job, 'I wish he would take a little more pride in his appearance.' The overriding truth about pride, nevertheless, is that it is dangerous as soon as it begins to lead to self-importance, as soon as it begins to look down on everyone else, as soon as it expects preferential treatment.

Of course some men, some women, are more capable or good looking than others. Only a fool would deny it. But what those accomplished people have to remember is that achievement is built on gifts; they cannot take even half the credit to themselves. The call to them is to remain humble, however healthy, wealthy or clever they may be. Pride goes before a fall, not least because it distorts true vision, not only of the self but of other people and of the environment. It is here that the danger of élitism lies. We need leaders in the community, even some men and women who are head and shoulders above the rest – the country requires them for its welfare – but if they become swell-headed, their value is diminished and they become a liability.

From the three occurrences of the saying of Jesus, 'For everyone who exalts himself will be humbled, and he who humbles himself will be exalted,' it is obvious that he condemned pride most strongly where it operates in the practice of religion – spiritual pride. The Pharisees were a glaring example in his day. He did not however fail to criticize pride in ordinary everyday life, in particular the persons who make it their aim always to obtain the front seats, bent not only on seeing but on being seen. The day will come when they will be humbled, if not always in this life but certainly in the next. Jesus, however, found *spiritual* pride the most offensive, the man or woman who gives the impression of being 'holier than thou' – the Catholic who despises the Evangelical lustily singing his hymns, and the Evangelical who cannot or will not recognize that the sacramentalist really has hold of the Christian message. We can be sure superior Christians of any sort are an abomination to Christ; their day of humbling will come, 'For everyone who exalts himself will be humbled, and he who humbles himself will be exalted,' and the clergy will not be excused. A hard saying, yes indeed, but no reader of the New Testament can complain that the warning has not been given.

5 JESUS THE SERVANT

What then should the Christian keep in mind? That this Jesus who gave the warning about pride, on occasions in unbelievably strong terms, the night before his crucifixion – indeed only a matter of hours before instituting the Eucharist – took a towel and wound it round himself, then took a basin, then a jar of water, and proceeded to wash his disciples' feet. This was the servants' task, and not a particularly attractive one. But Jesus humbled himself to this level. We Christians must be willing to act as servants to people. This is what we must keep in mind, then the sin of religious pride will have no dominion over us. We shall be able to hear Jesus saying with a measure of equanimity, 'For everyone who exalts himself will be humbled, and he who humbles himself will be exalted.'

22
THE FAMILY

If anyone comes to me and does not hate his father and mother, wife and children, brothers and sisters, even his own life, he cannot be a disciple of mine.
LUKE 14.26 (NEB)

I have chosen to preach on this saying of Jesus because as it stands it is repelling, we cannot believe that he uttered it, and this gives me the opportunity to speak about the style and manner of Jesus' teaching in general. It is nothing like a lecture or a chapter in a book. Jesus never wrote a book. In that sense there is no system in it. An index to it making possible the looking up of what he said on specific subjects is out of the question. All we have is reported sayings, most of them in answer to some question or arising out of an event, and which can only be understood by reference to the context. Because of this we must expect paradox, exaggeration, irony and parable. So his sayings become like popular proverbs which if taken literally may seem to contradict each other. This form, however, made the sayings memorable. My text today is an example: 'If anyone comes to me and does not hate his father and mother . . . he cannot be a disciple of mine.' Taken literally, it is nonsense. It is impossible therefore to 'pin Jesus down'. All of which means that the teaching of Jesus cannot be grasped by the intellect alone. It is not a subject we can 'get up'. It has to impinge on us in bits and pieces, and the bits and pieces have to lodge in the mind and feelings to reveal their significance as life goes on its way bumping into all manner of experience; then suddenly some saying of Jesus is illuminated and our reaction is, 'Oh, I see.' Maybe we find this tantalizing, but it is all we have, and we shall have to come to terms with it.

126

1 THE OCCASION OF THE SAYING

So we come to this saying in Luke 14.26. The occasion is surprising. Great crowds were accompanying Jesus and he turned to them and made this statement about hating the people closest to us, and even life itself, saying that this was necessary in order to be a disciple of his. We might perhaps have thought that such a saying might be more appropriately made in the close and intimate circle of the twelve disciples, if it were to be uttered at all. But no, it was called back to the crowds who were following on behind him. Was this then meant to be a jolt to people who were largely unthinking 'hangers on'? They were following him, yes, not least because of some of the benefit that might accrue in the way of healings and other startling occurrences, but the idea of a price did not enter their heads. So Jesus pitched it impossibly high: 'If anyone comes to me and does not hate his father and mother, wife and children, brothers and sisters, even his own life, he cannot be a disciple of mine.' We can only guess the look on the faces of the crowd who heard this.

2 THE MEANING OF THE SAYING

We turn now to enquire more exactly what the saying can mean. Matthew 10.37 helps us. There the saying is reported as being made not to the unreflective crowds following him who needed to be given a jolt, but to his twelve disciples about to be sent out on a mission. It reads: 'No man is worthy of me who cares more for father and mother than for me; no man is worthy of me who cares more for son or daughter; no man is worthy of me who does not take up his cross and walk in my footsteps.' Clearly the choice here is between natural affection and loyalty to Christ. In most cases they are not incompatible, but Christ's followers must

127

be ready, if the need arises, to act towards their loved ones *as if* they hated them. I can give an up-to-date illustration of this.

An up-to-date story is told of a father who wrote to his son to the effect that if he persisted in adhering to the Christian religion and the Christian community, considering all the care and money he had lavished on his upbringing he would have no other course but to count him as dead. He would never hear from him again. The son paid the price. He continued a Christian.

An unusual case? I don't know, but I guess something like it happens not only sometimes in Jewish families but in Islamic households as well. This is the point of Jesus' saying. If, I repeat, if a decision between love of parents and loyalty to Christ *has* to be made, to be a follower of Christ means an attitude to the parents has to be made *very like hatred*. Some Christians from non-Christian families have paid that terrible price.

3 FAMILY LOYALTY

I turn now to family loyalty. Jesus did not sit loosely to this. We must not forget that Jesus was born into a family. The gospels of St Matthew and St Luke almost bend over backwards to impress this on us. There are detailed genealogies. Jesus the Christ came from God, but he did not just appear on this earth. Virgin birth or no virgin birth (and I subscribe to the orthodox view, though well aware of the difficulties), Jesus, I repeat, did not just appear, he was born into a family. We shall be wise to reflect on this, especially today when family life is in decline. Jesus, to be what he was and came to be, needed the background of a family – father, mother, brothers and sisters. This is an astonishing thought, but there it is. Families make people what they are. As life progresses we have to move away from our families, and this includes ways of thinking, but not to break with them.

We can learn this from the story of Jesus. He began to move away at the age of twelve when he stayed behind in the Temple, causing his parents anxiety when they missed him. He gently rebuked his mother on two occasions when she attempted to interfere in his ministry, first at a marriage feast in Cana of Galilee and secondly when she attempted to get him home, away from the strain and stress of his public ministry. But he did not break from her. She followed him to the end and stood there by the cross. Jesus learned loyalty from childhood in a home and family. It is to be wondered if loyalty is not in short supply in our world today because of the break up of families. This is one of the sad consequences of the modern frequency of divorce, especially where there are children. A heavy price is paid by them and by society in general. Jesus honoured the family. Of course there are difficulties and tensions in family life, but they should be borne. Jesus' family was not ideal. His brothers, we are told, 'did not believe in him'. Perhaps it is not only loyalty that we learn in family life; we also learn there how to live with difficulties, and with tension and with atmosphere. The lesson is not to break with the family except as a last resort, when all else has been tried. And a small point, perhaps, but worth mentioning: when parents become aged and perhaps decrepit in body and mind, their family should visit them regularly – and this includes the man in the family, the women are more likely to turn up anyway.

Put all this together and it is obvious Jesus would never have counselled simply hating father, mother, wife and children, brothers and sisters on becoming a disciple of his. Furthermore, there came a day when he said to a group of Pharisees and lawyers from Jerusalem, 'God said, "Honour your father and your mother"' and 'The man who curses his father or mother must suffer death.' He was driven to these strong words when it came to his knowledge how these people tricked their parents in depriving them of money set apart for their benefit by saying it was set apart for God. Then of course they could get their hands on it. What hypocrisy, said Jesus. The truth surely is that parents and families should be honoured and supported readily and willingly, even when cost is involved.

All this that I have been saying about the family and its importance has taken us no doubt a long way from the saying of Jesus which it was my aim to expound, namely, 'If anyone comes to me and does not hate his father and mother, wife and children, brothers and sisters, . . . he cannot be a disciple of mine,' but we have come this long way in order to show how Jesus' use of the word 'hate' in the saying cannot be read in its literal sense, it should be read as 'cares more for father and mother than for me', as in Matthew 10.37.

Before I finish with this sensitive subject of the family, I would like to pay a tribute to those one-parent families where the woman inevitably has to carry the burden. It is sad and it is heavy, but not a few of these lonely women do their best for the children under their care, but it is a second best, yet they often achieve something very worthwhile. I speak with some feeling on this because in a way I come from a one-parent family, not through break-up but through death. My mother was left with two small boys, one aged six and the other (me) aged four. It was wartime. Money was short, food was short. But alone she struggled on, determined to do her best for her children. She found a church for us to attend (it had dropped out of her life, but she came with us), she found a school, she kept a watch on the other boys with whom we mixed. And both of us, my brother and I, made good. Credit is due to my mother in her one-parent family. I honour her. Credit must be due to many others today.

All this is passing. I end by reminding you of the nature of Jesus' way of teaching. It was in strong, challenging, often puzzling sayings, not easily understood at first, and in any case never understood by the intellect alone. One outstanding saying of this sort was the one I took for my text for this sermon today: 'If anyone comes to me and does not hate his father and mother, wife and children, brothers and sisters, even his own life, he cannot be a disciple of mine.' From this we can certainly carry away one conviction, Christ must be given priority in life.

23

GOD AND MONEY

*No servant can serve two masters: for either he will hate the
one, and love the other; or else he will hold to the one, and
despise the other. Ye cannot serve God and mammon.*

LUKE 16.13 (AV)

This saying of Jesus is reported in two places in the gospels
with precisely the same wording. I have chosen the Lukan
instance because the chapter where it occurs contains two
striking parables about money which call for comment; and
I have kept to the Authorized Version in my quotation
because this is the form most widely known. The New
English Bible version is interesting, but does not, I think,
outweigh the value of the familiarity of the old version.
Perhaps I ought to add that the word 'mammon' simply
means wealth.

I wonder if there was ever a time when more attention
was given to money than the present. Probably there was,
but with the advent of rapid dissemination of news and the
rising standard of living in the industrialized countries, more
people have more money, though there is still poverty,
so money is more talked about and is more the dominant
interest of people generally. And with the football pools and
the National Lottery more people are after it.

1 MONEY CAN BE DEMORALIZING

Now, is wealth a bad thing? Even to ask this question would
sound like the height of stupidity to many people. No, wealth
is not a bad thing, that is to say in itself, but the love of
money certainly is. 1 Timothy 6.10 (so often misquoted)

131

puts the matter plainly, 'For the love of money is the root of all evil', and the writer goes on, 'which while some coveted after, they have erred from the faith, and pierced themselves through with many sorrows.' So beware. Wealth can beguile. And do not imagine that only the wealthy can be 'hooked' on money, it can happen to the poor as well, they can judge everything in terms of money, perhaps with more excuse, wondering how they are going to pay their way, but the obsession is still corrupting.

Now let us go back to the context of the notable saying of Jesus about money in St Luke Chapter 16. When he said, 'No servant can serve two masters: for either he will hate the one, and love the other; or else he will hold to the one and despise the other. Ye cannot serve God and mammon,' the Pharisees, who, says the Scripture, loved money, 'scoffed at him'. Money was their guiding principle in life. What they should do or not do was decided upon the money involved. Will it pay to do this or will it pay to do that? The question of the rightness or wrongness of the alternative course of action did not enter into the matter. The deciding factor was the money involved in the alternatives. And this is the seriousness of the matter; in time, there comes about an inability to decide matters by anything other than money, indeed if there are other reasonable criteria at all. This is how and why the love of money is corrupting. It is demoralizing. Morals are demoted out of serious concern. In this situation God obviously has no place. Money is the controller; and compromise is impossible.

2 MONEY AND FALSE CONFIDENCE

And something else. It has to do with confidence for living in the ups and downs of life as we experience it. Where is our confidence based? Is it in our bank balance? I shall be all right. My assets are worth thousands. Jesus told a story about this (Luke 12.16–21). There was a rich man whose land produced bumper harvests, indeed so overwhelming was the volume of his produce he had to pull down his barns and build greater to house it all. And when it was all safely packed away he sat back. Those barns chock-a-block with goods were the ground of his confidence. Eat, drink and be merry! But God said to him, 'You fool, this very night you must surrender your life; you have made your money – who will get it now?' So perhaps we had better ask ourselves, where does our confidence for living lie? In our wealth? In our money? This is the seriousness of the matter. Where a person's confidence is placed determines the character of that person. Is it God? Or is it money? But we are only here because of God, his creative power and his sustaining power.

3 MONEY IS TO BE USED

This Chapter 16 of St Luke's gospel where my text occurs is mainly about money. It begins with a story and ends with a story. First a rich man who had a bailiff, but he was dishonest. He squandered his master's property. The rich man sent for him and told him he was giving him notice. Thoroughly alarmed, the bailiff set to making financial arrangements with his master's clients which would please them. Then, if and when he 'got the sack', these clients would look after him. All very subtle, all very cute, even if not quite 'above board'. But he had this to his credit. He didn't just sit on the money entrusted to him, *he used it* to good purpose, engaging his wits in the operation. An odd story, but there is a lesson. The people who have been entrusted with wealth (and it is a trust) had better not just sit on it, but use it for good causes, and 'heaven knows' there are plenty of those.

At the end of this Chapter 16 of St Luke's gospel is another story about a rich man. Indeed he flaunted his wealth, living in luxury while at the gate of his mansion there lay a wretched creature, called Lazarus, penniless and covered with sores who would have been glad of the scraps from the rich man's table. But the rich man took no notice. He did not use his money even for the 'good cause' on his doorstep. He will pay for that hardness of heart in life beyond this life. He had blatantly failed to use his money. So he had become hard. Money does this unless it is used for good and needy causes. Money lovers are hard people. We become like the things we love, and if money is the predominant love then there can be no doubt about the dire consequence. The only safeguard is to use money, but not for oneself alone.

4 WE MUST LEARN TO LIVE WITH MONEY

The Christian, then, is not required to go penniless. He/she is not called to go about in rags and live in a hovel. Some, like St Francis of Assisi, have been set apart to a life of extreme poverty. We are not all made to this, indeed very few are, and those who respond faithfully are to be honoured. Theirs is a remarkable witness. Wealthy Christians, however – and they do exist – are called to a modest style of living, they are not to flaunt their wealth and they should make it their business to be humble in manner and approachable, willing to meet with anybody.

Come back to my text, the saying of Jesus, 'No servant can serve two masters . . . you cannot serve God and mammon.' But we shall have to live with mammon. Mammon is round every corner. The first necessity therefore for the wealthy Christian is to *dethrone money* and keep it dethroned. It is not a god and it is not to be regarded as a god. Money may be, and often is, dirty, and if we are not careful we shall be dirtied by it. Perhaps it is in this area of life we stand in greatest need of God's cleansing power. We can be tempted to sin by money, and often are. Money is a terrible tempter. Let us be warned, let us be careful, but let us know that we can be kept from falling, and if we fall, God will not cast us off if we humbly seek the grace of his forgiveness. Money is a sensitive area of life. We need to be on our guard.

Perhaps I could sum up all this in one simple sentence. Let us as Christians be charitable people and we shall be safe from this particular snare, whatever our bank balance.

24
LOST AND SAVED

For the Son of man came to seek and to save the lost.
LUKE 19.10 (RSV)

We all like to hear stories about people, especially of course people we know or who are prominent 'in the news'. This is one of the reasons why obituary notices occupy a regular place in the newspapers. They do not only record the death of the person but a summary of his/her life; where the person came from, the family background and how there was a striking rise to a position of eminence, and of course a line or two about marriage. I mention this because today, in opening up another of the famous sayings of Jesus, I am able to attach it directly to a story about a person which makes it come alive very quickly. The saying is, 'For the Son of man came to seek and to save the lost,' and the person in connection with whom it was uttered is Zacchaeus. The story is in Luke 19.1–10.

1 ZACCHAEUS THE TAX COMMISSIONER

We know what he looked like. He was a little man and, since he was rich and no doubt well-fed, probably a bit portly. But he could run and was not averse to doing so, though the sight must have been slightly comic, but that didn't worry him. He was a chief tax-collector, that is to say not a taxman like Levi, who sat in his grubby little office down by the Lake of Galilee taking 'a rake off' from all who had crossed the lake carrying merchandise. His story is in Luke 5.27. No,

136

this man was probably a commissioner of taxes, overseeing quite a number of ordinary tax-gatherers; he did not handle the dirty coins himself. He controlled the tax business in Jericho, a city not only beautifully but also strategically situated in a main trade route. Much of the produce of the whole area had to pass through it. Not surprisingly, then, this man, Zacchaeus, was rich; in short, he was a rich Jew doing well for himself, and no doubt living very comfortably. We may be sure he knew 'on which side his bread was buttered', as we say, but there is nothing to indicate that he was thoroughly corrupt, thoroughly bad; on the contrary, he was a respectable official in an important city, the gateway to the capital, Jerusalem. All in all, not only in mileage but also in style, a long way from Galilee.

He wanted to see Jesus, which means that he must have heard a great deal about him and was intrigued. And the day came when crowds of people were evidently passing through Jericho, making plenty of noise, no doubt, after the way of crowds. Zacchaeus pricked up his ears, and when on enquiry he was told that Jesus was passing through he recognized his chance to see him; unfortunately, though, the chance for him was minimal because the crowds would block his view, not least because of the smallness of his stature. But knowing the road Jesus and the crowd must take, he visualized precisely where he would find a vantage point. It was just outside the city, where trees lined the route, fig-mulberry trees, not unlike the English oak, with many lateral branches, easy to climb and much planted to give shade along roadways. Zacchaeus saw his chance, so he ran. People in the crowd saw him running, all so undignified, and then actually climb one of the trees. I cannot believe they did not shout out rude remarks with his name attached, but Zacchaeus knew what he wanted and was used to getting it, and in any case he was, as a taxman, not unfamiliar with rudeness. So there he is, perched up in a tree by the roadside in Jericho.

And now the crunch point in the story. When Jesus and the crowd swarming all around him reached that point on the road, he stopped, fair and square in front of Zacchaeus up in the tree. Zacchaeus could see all right, but what he did not expect was Jesus' address to him plain and clear, 'Zacchaeus.' Yes, he called him by name, picked up I guess from the jeering crowd, 'Zacchaeus, make haste and come down; for I must stay at your house today.' Zacchaeus could scarcely believe his ears. But there was no hesitation. He came down immediately and received Jesus joyfully, his face all smiles. And to the utter astonishment of the bystanders, they saw the door of Zacchaeus' house opened and Jesus received inside – actually across the threshold, just like an honoured guest. One overall comment rose to the lips of the dumbfounded watching bystanders, not about Zacchaeus but about Jesus: 'He has gone in to be the guest of a man who is a sinner.' It was shocking. Decent people did not entertain taxmen, and certainly the religious wouldn't touch them. But the drama was not quite over. Zacchaeus appeared through his own door, and facing the crowds made a public statement addressed to Jesus, calling him Lord, 'Behold, Lord, the half of my goods I give to the poor; and if I have defrauded any one of anything, I restore it fourfold.' Had there been any newspapers as in our day, we can be certain this would have been reported in heavy type on the front page. Taxmen did not give the half of their goods to the poor or agree to make fourfold restoration for any fraudulent action. But Zacchaeus made this public promise, and Jesus responded, 'Today salvation has come to this house, since he also is a son of Abraham.' And then this, which has become a famous saying, 'For the Son of man came to seek and to save the lost.'

So was Zacchaeus, for all his wealth, eminent position in Jericho and unquestionable respectability, lost? He certainly seemed to have been found by his contact with Jesus. He was a different man at once, open to people, generous, ready to help and willing to admit his faults. What a day that was when he climbed the fig-mulberry tree by the roadside. Would he ever forget it? Would the people in Jericho ever stop talking about it?

2 INTEREST IN THE MAN JESUS

But we have some questions to ask. How did Jesus know that that man up the tree would respond positively when he said, 'Zacchaeus, make haste and come down; for I must stay at your house today'? He might have reacted with sullenness, hostility or even offensiveness. But Jesus read him, he saw up the tree a man not only wealthy and successful, but one for whom life was meaningless and without inner satisfaction, a man with the not infrequent remark on his lips, 'What is the point of it all, all this success of mine, all this authority in Jericho, all this comfort? To what does it add up?' In that way he was lost. He didn't know where he was going, he had no direction in his life, it was simply a whole series of one thing after another; today's phrase would be 'one damned thing after another'. Jesus was concerned, is concerned, about that kind of person, and they are not out of date, they exist in plenty in the successful, comfortable, respectable areas of our modern world. What is the point of our hectic business?

I invite you to notice that this profoundly shattering experience of Zacchaeus all began with simple interest in Jesus obtained through hearsay. Jesus' words and deeds intrigued him. He must know more. This reinforces what I have tried to emphasize before. It is the duty of the preacher, the prime duty of the evangelist, to give people the opportunity to see Jesus and to hear his sayings. And to do it so that he arouses interest. And for this reason that spiritual experience and Christian discipleship with all the attendant care and concern for others can begin, and often does begin, in simply being intrigued by the man Jesus of Nazareth. Certainly this is the place to begin with children, but not only with them. If adults are intrigued by him they may not climb up a tree to see him, but they will certainly not let the experience go, and may grow as a result into strong Christian men and women. So the message for the Church in every age is to proclaim Jesus, let people see him, make him real to them.

139

How did Jesus know that Zacchaeus would respond to him? He had not met him before. Was it simply that astonishing ability of Jesus to read people at a glance? There are instances of this in the gospels. Did he see Zacchaeus running up the roadside and reason that no well-dressed official would be doing that unless he were sincere and in earnest? Or was this a case of miraculous insight on the part of the incarnate Word of God? Who can be certain what is the right answer? But what is clear is that Jesus saw not only a taxman running, he saw a lost man, and it was such that he came to save from meaninglessness in life. Hence his saying capping this event, 'For the Son of man came to seek and to save the lost.' My view is that he deliberately chose to enter the house of a rich tax-gatherer to demonstrate his unwillingness to write anyone off, great or small sinner though he be in the popular estimation.

3 THE CRUCIFIXION THE CLIMAX

I hope I do not let my imagination run away with me, but I cannot forget that Zacchaeus received Jesus into his house about a week before he was crucified. When Jesus passed through Jericho he was on his way to the road leading up to Jerusalem, and there he was nailed to a cross, the most cruel form of execution ever invented. Zacchaeus would have heard of this. Everyone in Jerusalem and beyond heard of it. It was meant to be crudely public, and it was. To a few people it gave intense satisfaction, to the majority dismay and bewilderment. Many returned from the crucifixion site beating their breasts. How did the news, or even possibly the sight, affect Zacchaeus? Who can possibly know? But this is certain, however deeply any man or woman is intrigued by Jesus, they cannot hold him in their sight without the crucifixion. At the end of the day, when thankfully we grasp the truth that we receive salvation when we receive Jesus into our lives as Zacchaeus received him into his house, and that the Son of man came specifically to seek and save the lost, we have to know that that horrible crucifixion was his saving act. It was not extorted from him. It was his willing sacrifice for our salvation. Christ is *our crucified Saviour*. He saves from the cross.